W9-AAL-274

❧ ❧ ❧

In Praise
of Our Teachers

Also by Gloria Wade Gayles

Father Songs: Testimonies
by African-American Sons and Daughters

Rooted Against the Wind: Personal Essays

Pushed Back to Strength:
A Black Woman's Journey Home

My Soul Is a Witness: African-American
Women's Spirituality

Anointed to Fly

No Crystal Stair: Race and Sex
in Black Women's Novels, 1946–1976

❧ ❧ ❧

In Praise
of Our Teachers

❧ ❧ ❧

A Multicultural Tribute
to Those Who Inspired Us

Edited by Gloria Wade Gayles

BEACON PRESS   Boston

Beacon Press
25 Beacon Street
Boston, Massachusetts 02108–2892
www.beacon.org

Beacon Press books
are published under the auspices of
the Unitarian Universalist Association of Congregations.

Printed in the United States of America

07 06 05 04 03   8 7 6 5 4 3 2 1

This book is printed on acid-free paper that meets
the uncoated paper ANSI/NISO specifications
for permanence as revised in 1992.

Text design by Melodie Wertelet/mwdesign

Composition by Wilsted & Taylor Publishing Services

Library of Congress Cataloging-in-Publication Data

In praise of our teachers : a multicultural tribute to those
who inspired us / edited by Gloria Wade Gayles.
      p. cm.
   ISBN 0-8070-3148-8
   1. Teacher-student relationships—United States—
Anecdotes. 2. Teachers—United States—Anecdotes.
3. Students—United States—Biography.
I. Wade Gayles, Gloria Jean.
LB1033.I49 2003
371.1—dc21

                         2002066686

for our teachers

Contents

Introduction

> *Have you ever really had a teacher? One who saw you as a raw but precious thing, a jewel that, with wisdom, could be polished to a proud shine? If you are lucky enough to find your way to such teachers, you will always find your way back.*
> ❧ Mitch Albom, *Tuesdays with Morrie*

My elementary school and my high school were a fifteen- to twenty-minute walk from my unit in the Foote Homes Housing Project, which was a short distance from historic Beale Street in Memphis, Tennessee. In appearance, the schools seemed to be extensions of the projects, their red bricks similar to the red bricks of individual housing units. My elementary school stood in vigilant watch as my peers and I crossed the wide and busy boulevard that separated the flag-topped structure from the hundreds of units in which we lived, claiming us and calling us inside. When we reached the boulevard, we had no reason to look to the right or left for passing cars. On the projects side, a student wearing the coveted yellow patrol belt held us back until traffic cleared. On the school side, a smiling teacher directed us to the school building, reminding us in a comforting voice to walk quietly in single file down the long sidewalk through the open doors to our assigned homerooms.

In contrast to the projects' parquet floors, sometimes covered with inexpensive linoleum that dulled and cracked after a short period of use, the floors in both my elementary school and my high school were hardwood, polished to a shine and kept that way throughout the day by women and men who walked ceremoniously up and down the halls, stroking the floors with long-handled dust mops. On either side of the long and wide hall of polished floors, a row of wooden doors beckoned to us, bearing in very large readable letters teachers' names and homeroom designations. Each year, from first through twelfth grades, whenever I opened my homeroom door, I would immediately see a large and colorful bulletin board, its theme, colors, and cutouts varying from month to month. To be chosen to stay after school and change the boards was a cherished privilege. We would take down the old boards, handling each cardboard display and silver thumbtack with care, and put up the new boards, arranging colorful cutouts as the teacher directed, sometimes standing on chairs to reach beyond our young heights. When I would learn later in college that Aristotle believed our senses are nonintegrative units, acting independently of one another, I would think about these large colorful bulletin boards that touched all of our senses at the same time. We could smell, hear, and feel the text of that which we saw, that which decorated the world our teachers made for us.

I valued the bulletin boards, but I remember even more, in a special way, the chalkboards. They ran the full length of the front of each classroom, forming a majestic backdrop for the teacher in charge. To be chosen to write on the chalkboard was also a cherished privilege. With a dust eraser close at hand, we wrote, as the teacher directed, page numbers for homework, quotes for the day, or the names of students who were tardy or who had paid for field trips. We were careful in our work to leave undisturbed any information the teacher had written before our arrival. We knew this information was very important because underneath it, in yellow chalk, the teacher had written four words and underlined them twice: PLEASE DO NOT ERASE.

Those four words could well be a subtitle for this anthology, for the contributors herein bear witness to the impact teachers have had on their lives. They journey into clear memory where their experiences with committed and creative teachers reside, never to be erased. Whether the experience took place in rural Mississippi or northern Massachusetts, in the first grade or in college, in an English class or a science class, the contributors—from varying races, ethnicities, and persuasions—praise their teachers for guiding them to paths they would not have traveled otherwise. This is a special and unique anthology in that it shows teachers directly touching the lives of individuals and indirectly affecting the world at large. College presidents and professors, high school administrators, scholars, actors, artists, ministers, therapists—all of the contributors attribute their choice of profession, their achievements, and even their view of the world to a teacher's early influence. Each writer shares with us the answer to the question we all must ask ourselves: How did I become who I am and what I am?

For each contributor, the answer is the same: A teacher believed in them, a teacher taught with passion and depth, a teacher inspired with patience and love, a teacher mentored with compassion, a teacher pushed them and held them to high standards so that they would realize their highest selves. When I ask myself how and why I became a teacher, I recall the names of those who influenced my life: Annette Hubbard Roberts, Mary Alice McWilliams, Velma McLemore, Juanita Williamson, and Lionel Arnold. They showed me not only the joy of learning and the joy of teaching, but also, and perhaps more important, they taught me by example that only a thin, all-but-invisible line separates the two experiences: Those who teach also learn.

I Saw Them Believing

When I reflect on my favorite teachers . . . they were teachers who were my friends, too. I see teachers wearing many titles besides teacher. I see psychologist, mother, father, friend, and adviser.
శ్రీ Ennis Cosby

𝔅 *From a Conversation with*
Audrey Forbes Manley

B ased on my own experiences in rural Mississippi in the late 1940s, I believe teachers are miracle workers who can dramatically change the course of our lives. Often they are the last lifeline children have, the one straight line to self-esteem, dreams, and success. I will be eternally grateful to three of my teachers: Miss Fraser, Miss Owen, and especially Mr. Caldwell. He taught me math and science in seventh through ninth grades. At a time when it was unheard of for a poor Black girl in rural Mississippi to believe she could do math, Mr. Caldwell convinced me that I could. He was tough, exacting, and challenging. Because he believed in me, I did everything I could to live up to his high expectations. I can honestly say Mr. Caldwell influenced me early in life to set my course on science and become a physician.

I want to put my arms around these teachers and others who were a part of my education and training. I would like to give them a big hug and tell them, again and again, "Thank you." But they deserve more than words. I think the best way any of us can thank our teachers is to show them what we have done with the gifts they gave us and share those gifts with others.

Ю Deborah J. G. James

Learning to Be Heard:
Portrait of Teacher Sister Dolorosa, O.S.P.

"*Somebody get me my music out of the cupboard.*"

"*I'm not going in that cupboard. You get it!*" hisses the girl across from me. We are both in the back row nearest the cupboard.

"*I'm not going anywhere near that cupboard!*" The panic rising in me makes my stage whisper squeaky. "*You know you can't find nothing in that cupboard!*"

"*I said somebody get me my* music *out of that* cupboard!" Sister Dolorosa's voice carries the impending storm. Feet shuffle. Nervous bodies shift in the student desks. People gesture and hiss at Janice and me to get the music! But we are frozen. Everybody knows the closet is a disaster area. No one could ever find anything in there that he or she is sent to find. The price of looking but coming up empty-handed is the public humiliation of being called "Dumb bugga!" in front of everyone, despite the fact that everyone in the room had already received this honor on more than one occasion, collectively and individually.

So we hesitate. A fraction too long. The human whirlwind is bearing down on us—the black habit inflated by the gust of wind she creates as she sails toward us. She flings open the door to the cupboard and begins tossing out all manner of workbooks and supplies as she hunts down the sheet music she has been calling for, muttering about our general incompetence. Or is it our disobedience? But as soon as she lays hands on the sought-for music, she emerges, like sunshine from behind a cloud, flashing her single dimple and *exposing the gap between her front teeth. We all smile because we know the storm is over. Sister Dolorosa holds no grudges and her storms, while intense, pass quickly. Anyway, we are getting ready for the best part of every day—music.*

♣

I recall that Sister Dolorosa had a rich singing voice, with an impressive range full of what I learned much later is called tonal color. Perhaps more important, she had the gift of charming out of us multipart harmonies for a wide array of music styles (from "Lift Every Voice and Sing" to the complete sound track of *The Sound of Music*). Her voice cushioned ours and called out to us for an equal response. Sometimes she would pit a whole section—altos, second sopranos—against her singing of a complementary part, and she would hold her own against our multiple voices. It was a technique she used to urge us into full voice. "Come on!" she would say. "You can't let one person out-sing all of you." And we would suck in air, throw our heads back, and sing. "But sweetly now. No yelling. We're making *music* here." That's what flowed out of her like her laughter—music. Then there was her energy. It seemed to me that ordinary verbs didn't apply to Sister Dolorosa. She strode or dashed. And where she strode, life bloomed.

That energy served her well. She was the principal of Our Lady of Consolation Catholic School, a mission school (although we were not much aware of this at the time) for African-American children in Charlotte, North Carolina. Sister Dolorosa—though she was Mother Dolorosa then—somewhere in her early thirties probably, was the person in charge of the team of Oblate Sisters of Providence (a historically Black order of sisters whose Mother House is in Baltimore, Maryland). Sister, and the women who came with her, took their mission work seriously. They were intent on "doing God's work" and changing the world.

During my time with Sister Dolorosa (and through her voice that has been internalized in me in all the years since), she guided me and my classmates—pushing and pulling, celebrating and encouraging, reprimanding and chiding. Hers was not always the gentle touch of today's "nurturers," but she intended for us all to go as high as we could, to make the most of whatever talents we might have. At a time when most of us were seeking to "blend" (seventh and eighth grade), she was always discovering traits that set a person apart and saying those things out loud. Sister Dolorosa first "named" me into the world beyond my circle of family and friends. Although she was certainly not the first one to speak to me and my classmates about our responsibility to the world, she was the first to make *me* hear that I had gifts that impelled those responsibilities.

"Somebody in this room is not living up to her potential." We all stopped whatever desk work we had been doing and looked up. This was one of her "talks." Like the rest of my classmates, I looked around the room with mild curiosity.

"You would be surprised at the test scores this young lady has, given the way she works." Again, like my classmates, I had my own ideas of who had "good test scores." It must have been Lynne or Joanne or Karen. Maybe it was even Gwen. She was really nice and seemed smart enough. But we knew Sister well enough to know we wouldn't be held in suspense long.

"You, Miss Grier. According to these scores, you should be doing much higher-level work." I was flabbergasted. Me? I was an average Black girl, with average intelligence, working on having "personality" because my grandmother, among others, had let me know gently that my fortune was not in my looks. So I needed to hear that I had gifts. But Sister made sure everyone understood that along with gifts came responsibilities beyond personal pleasure and profit.

Her encouragement was matter of fact—"Deborah, you like to write poems. I'm tired of those verses we sing at eleven o'clock mass. We need something new by this Friday. Write some new ones." I had never even attempted to write lyrics for songs, let alone hymns. Weren't they "holy"? Didn't they come directly from the Holy Spirit? But I knew even less about how you said "no" to Sister Dolorosa. After all, she was my teacher, my principal, and a nun—wouldn't God strike me down if I willfully disobeyed her? So I tried. I had written *something* by Friday—miserable and thin though it was, we used it (only once). The important things were her faith that I *would* write something and my effort not to let her down. We were all afraid of her, afraid of her scorn, afraid of her anger, but mostly afraid of her possible contempt. Likewise, we were warmed in deep places by her approval.

Some of her most powerful teaching was by example. She threw herself into whatever work was at hand, getting the bathrooms cleaned or preparing us for a concert. I never saw her hesitate to tackle getting whatever she thought her kids needed. "It would certainly be nice if we could have some more of those notebooks (or apples, or whatever, fill in the blank). But we can't afford any more." Sighing, the storekeeper would say, "Well, Sister, how many more do you need?" A smiling Sister Dolorosa would say, "Not too many more." Then she would direct whichever students she had brought with her to help her carry out the booty. We always shook our heads a little in pity for the poor outmatched storekeeper.

Teaching opportunities were never lost either. If we needed costumes for the operetta (of course we Black children staged a "Japanese" operetta, wearing faintly Hawaiian-print costumes—but colorful—and singing in English), she found someone to help us learn to choose and sew the cloth as well as to teach us the music, the lines, the movements. We learned to do both manual and academic labor. Many of the guys from her classes still laugh about learning to handle the big buffer for the floors as well as learning to talk about history. We did that work not only because we could not say "no" to her, but also because we understood without her telling us that we would need to be prepared to do whatever was necessary to survive in the world. What she *did* tell us clearly and explicitly was that we would have to work twice as hard as our white counterparts to do as well as them. So we practiced twice as long for the annual Glee Club concert; we learned the multipart harmonies and sang till our heads rang and we were nearly sick. But *we* knew, before the applause and shouts that signaled approval, that we had done well, in fact, better even than the high school students who followed us. She made us sweat, but we reaped the rewards of our labor.

It was not in Sister Dolorosa to back away from a challenge nor to let us do so. One morning she swept into the classroom and said, "Deborah Grier, you are going to represent us in the Diocesan Oratorical Contest." My first thought was, "What's an oratorical?" She explained to the whole class that it was a speech contest, that I was to write a speech on a specified topic and practice my delivery in class. I was afraid; I had never done this kind of public speaking before. It went without saying that the judges would all be white and that my competition would probably also be white, since we were the only Black school in the diocese. The only chance I would have was to be much, much better prepared than my opponents. So I worked on that speech every day for at least a month, and every day for at least two weeks before the contest, I practiced it in front of my class-mates until in the final days, they actually all said the speech aloud with me, mimicking my hand gestures and inflections.

Two days before the event, Sister Dolorosa made me stand before the class for an inspection. I would be wearing my school uniform; mine was fading from the sharp navy blue to a purple hue from washing and my white collar was a bit frayed. So she directed a classmate to loan me her uniform —newer, brighter, a better fit. As I look back on it, I might have been embarrassed by this public sizing up and the way in which Sister ordered us to switch. Perhaps the donor was. What I remember is the sense of battle planning. What would it take for us to win? We were, all of us, involved; this was no solitary effort. The whole class was directed to be present at the competition, in uniform and on time. That was also the way we attended basketball games—everyone there, in uniform and on time, and we cheered and stomped our support for the team, no matter what. (I was secretly relieved. Since everyone knew my part so well, if the worst happened and I should faint or something, any one of them could complete the speech for me.) We arrived in force.

All I remember of that performance is a rush of energy and a flailing of my arms to emphasize my points. When my mem-ory seemed about to slip from me, I looked out into the audi-ence to the blue and white bank of Black faces turned toward me and breathed again into the performance. Just seeing them there, flanked by Sister in her black and white (Why does my memory always have her standing straight up?), not only beat back the rising panic but let me ride out the end of my speech on a crest of energy. We took home the second-place trophy, but for me the victory was in experiencing the group effort that supported me individually and the clear sense that my talents and my successes were not mine alone.

Sister Dolorosa was a complicated woman who inspired complicated, contradictory feelings and great passion. Even today, no two people carry the same memories of our time with her. What was bracing for some of us was simply harsh for others. But for me she remains a vivid image of dedication, intelligence, humor, and heart. Her touch was not always gentle, but her intent never varied. Her goal was to squeeze, pull, tease, deliver from us the best that was there. In doing that, she made me aware of possibility and imprinted me with her energy and strength.

⚷ Lydia Cortes

In Praise of Good
Teachers, with Love

Praising teachers is not second nature to me. I look back—
in anger at times?—on my education in the public schools
of New York City from the late 1940s to 1963, and there were,
unfortunately, few teachers worthy of praise or admiration.
There were many more that engendered in me, in the absence
of admiration, very little positive reaction at all. The majority
of my teachers did not help in creating a viable learning space.
Worse, school for me was an unwelcoming, discomfort-filled
place. From elementary through high school, with rare excep-
tions, I felt as if I did not belong. It was a place I had no other
choice than to endure. I had to do the time. Perhaps that is why
the exceptional teachers—those who were accepting, motivating, caring, and loving—stand out in my mind. These teachers have secured a special spot in my heart even after so many
years.

I started school at the age of five when I entered kindergarten at P.S. 55. The elementary school was located in the
Williamsburg section of Brooklyn. Back then the population
of Williamsburg was a combination of both Hasidic and non-
Hasidic Jews, some Italians, and the beginnings of a Puerto
Rican population that would in the 1950s come to dominate
the area.

That first morning of school my mother held my hand,
squeezing it tightly as we left our apartment, descended the
six flights of stairs, and walked the five or so blocks to P.S. 55.

There was something different, an apprehension of some sort transmitted through the tremors of my mother's hand, even if consciously I did not know what I was feeling. Actually, I think that feeling of amorphous unease had been present for days. That morning, Mami's anxiety was exaggerated, highlighted by her actions and words as she went about preparing for my first day in school. She tied the bows at the end of my braids and the laces on my shoes repeatedly, each time more tightly. She hovered over me, urging me to hurry and eat, nervously watching to make sure I chewed and swallowed each bite of my breakfast. My mother may have tried to give me some kind of orientation for school, about what I could expect, but I honestly do not remember any of that. In any case, she probably did not know much of what went on in American schools, having only attended a few schools as a child in Puerto Rico.

My initial impression of that first morning in school was made as soon as Mami pulled open the heavy metal door of the building: School smells. The various scents assaulted me. I almost gagged, and Mami nodded and wrinkled her nose in acknowledgment. However, despite the stench, she leaned against the door with the weight of her body to hold it open, motioning for me to go inside. The air was a sickening combination of decomposing cafeteria food—orange peels and onions and vegetable soup. Hanging above it all, there was an additional layer—the smell of disinfectants (King Pine and bleach), probably meant to cover up the faint but still present stink of vomit. Even today, walking into most public schools in New York City, that smell invades my nostrils, an odor that, in my head and gut, will always be associated with schools. It is similar to the connection I make with other dreaded institutional places like public hospitals and old-age homes—other places where people are confined.

The other thing I remember from that first day was my mother's sense of discomfort—or shame?—that seemed to be magnified by the patronizing attitudes of many of the people in the school, attitudes that were manifested in their demeanor, the way we were looked at or dismissed. I remember experiencing peculiar, distressful feelings, although at the time I had no words for them, even in Spanish. In fact, for many years to come, I did not summon up those feelings or in any way verbalize them. Unknowingly, I had buried them deep inside, as if the treatment my mother and I received that day was deserved somehow and therefore the shame we had felt needed to be concealed forever.

Mami had learned English in school in her hometown of Ponce and spoke it fairly well, albeit with an accent. She was shy and somewhat withdrawn and sometimes felt ashamed of or self-conscious about her accent, sometimes—such as those times when certain people asked her to repeat whatever she had said, for whatever their reason. Later on, when I knew more English and more about people and life in general, I wondered if those people had really misunderstood her or if they had asked her to repeat her utterances to make fun of her accent, of her. Before she would let the words out again, Mami would always turn red, eyes fixed down. When the words did come, they were even more belabored, her accent perhaps thickened with the glue of embarrassment. A few years later, when I was able to speak an accent-free English (over the years, however, my Spanish suffered for lack of sufficient use), I realized that Mami's way of speaking was unique; I realized what an accent was in the first place and that she had one. And I was a bit ashamed, for I was made to understand that such an accent was "un-American." Mami's pronunciation was affected by Spanish phonetics. For example, she said *ve-ge-table* so you heard the word *table* in it. Cafeteria was turned into a *café* (with the accent on the *fe*) and the *te* and *ria* tacked on the end. Now I think of her accent as charming and somewhat childlike, as she was in so many ways.

Nevertheless, on that first day of school, as on the many days that followed, I did not speak English. I had never attended any kind of school, and the only children I knew and played with, other than my sister and brother, were my cousins or the children of my family's friends. We all spoke in Spanish. Therefore, I could not understand the teacher's brief words as she came out of the kindergarten class and approached Mami in the hallway. I could not understand the few words she said to my mother as she waved Mami away as one might a pesky fly. I couldn't fully understand but clearly remember the terror I felt when Mami let go of my hand and turned me over to the teacher. I couldn't understand why the teacher put her arm around my shoulders as if to protect me but then prodded me into her classroom. Although I could understand my mother's words of good-bye, her hug and kiss, I did not understand why she would leave me in the first place. I could not make any sense of it, even after Mami whispered for me not to worry, that time would pass quickly and before I knew it she would be back to get me and we could go home. I remember how slowly each day after that one moved. I often wanted to stay home and, just as frequently, Mami had to convince me that I really wanted to be in school, that I needed to be there.

Then along came Miss Powell, the first teacher I loved, the first in my public school student life whom I found praiseworthy. My memory of Miss Powell overflows with her kindnesses, her grace, her beauty, her goodness. Even after fifty years (can it really be that so many years have passed?), my affection for her is still strong. I always felt her love for me. Miss Powell was the one who taught me English, but in reality, she taught me so much more. I don't remember if I had her in first or second grade. I do remember that she was always happy with my successes, no matter how small they might have seemed to others or even to me. Love was there every time I struggled to use a new word, whenever I tried to put words together to make a sentence, every time I was able to capture the meaning of her questions so I could attempt to answer them. She did not expect perfection from me, but she inspired me with her love and acceptance to reach ever higher toward the next plateau.

Miss Powell was beautiful. In truth, her forehead may have been too wide, her eyes not large enough, her lips too thin to be considered a conventional beauty back then or even now. But to me she was absolutely gorgeous, as doubtless she must have seemed to the other students fortunate enough to have had her as their teacher. Her real beauty, I now realize, lay in her abilities as a fine and loving teacher, a fine and loving person. She made me feel good. She made me feel smart. I *was* smart . . . with her, for her. She encouraged me to take chances even if I made "mistakes." I remember wanting to do the best I could for her because she believed in me. Come to think of it, that is the one characteristic that all of my praiseworthy teachers had in common, no matter how different they may have been in other ways. They all believed in their students. They didn't give up on them by citing excuses or make premises based on stereotypes or erect barriers and roadblocks to learning. They didn't say that "these" kids can't learn because of a host of reasons: the overwhelming poverty of certain neighborhoods or the lack of formal education in their families, or that their parents "don't care" or their lack of English language skills, and on and on.

With her brilliant smiles, her welcoming gestures, her

sense of humor, Miss Powell encouraged me, spurred me on, gave me permission to take chances, the risks necessary for real learning. She didn't have the constant need to be conferring words of praise on her students—the "goods," "very goods," or "excellents" that some teachers use so liberally and insincerely, not realizing that most of their students know exactly how *good* they are at something. Miss Powell's accolades were always there, but they were all rolled up in her teacher self, like the jelly in a jelly roll, implied in her manner, in her bearing, in her gaze. She never held back her words of kindness or support; they were as highly cherished as she was. I loved her. I wanted to be just like her when I grew up.

Miss Powell made it possible for me to learn to say *shirt* instead of *chirt*, *cheek* for *sheek*, *ship* for *chip* and *chip* for *ship*, *aren't* for *ain't*, *toilet paper* for *paper toilet*. She taught me English, but never at the expense of my native tongue. She taught me that speaking Spanish was just as good as speaking English. She taught me the value of knowing both languages. Miss Powell asked me to teach her some words in Spanish and made a fuss about my being able to say things another way. She asked questions about the food my family liked and beamed when I brought her some Mami had sent. Her smile broadened after she took her first forkful of the tasty rice and beans, her first bite of a fried plantain. Miss Powell made it possible for me to expand my knowledge of English, but more important, through my experience with her, she made it possible for me to expand my perceptions and attitudes about teachers, about what learning really can be. I came to understand that you can learn another language and about another culture without being expected to ridicule or reject the one you came into at birth. I learned that some teachers could be interested enough in me to learn about me and from me and to appreciate my world, my language, my culture. And that made it safe for me to appreciate the other world, theirs.

⅌

A few years later, in fifth grade, I developed an immediate crush on my teacher Mr. Seidman. He was young, had wavy light brown hair, dark blue eyes, and a soft, calming, reassuring voice. Eventually all the children loved him. Even on the first day he didn't have the need to resort to the "You want to see how mean I can really get" demeanor many teachers often used to "establish law and order, to establish the rules." To establish that they were, in fact, running the whole show and could therefore withhold any goodies, any favors—even going to the bathroom—any time they wanted to because "This is my classroom and I'm the only boss."

Mr. Seidman did have classroom rules, but he involved us all in making them and we discussed why or if they were necessary in the first place. He talked about some of the projects that he had planned for us, projects that involved us actively in thinking, in making decisions. Up until then, I thought a project was just a word for the high-rise, often dangerous buildings with the stinky elevators where people poorer than my immediate family—like my cousins and my Tio Alfredo—lived. Mr. Seidman's projects had to do with building *terrariums,* or going to visit museums or places in the *community.* We would work in *committees* to *present* what we had learned, and we had choices in how we did it, as long as we made it comprehensible to the rest of the class. We acted out our knowledge through little plays, through murals, through song and dance, through reports delivered with photographs; we made believe we were newscasters, weather forecasters, guides. There were so many ways of learning, and it was almost too much fun, even sinful, to be learning in these ways. This was not what I had come to think learning was supposed to be.

By the fifth grade I was painfully shy and afraid to have any attention drawn to me. I had been taught well to fear making mistakes in school. I feared the possible ridicule of the other children, if not that of the teachers. I feared looking stupid. I feared that I might be stupid. And yet part of me wanted to shine, wanted the spotlight, wanted the attention, the "applause," the approval I had seen less shy children receive when they put themselves on "stage." But would I ever admit to wanting any of that? It was too scary. What if I failed? It could be the end of the world—my world as I perceived it back then. I wonder why I took things so very seriously, always believing the worst was about to occur, that the best was impossible to achieve, so why try?

The why of trying came less than halfway through fifth grade with Mr. Seidman. Our class was involved in yet another project—a play about teeth and the importance of taking good care of them. Mr. Seidman even got permission for us to visit the office of a real dentist—a friend of his from his undergraduate college days. The whole class, as was usual, would participate in the actual production and presentation of the play. Some of the kids would draw and paint the scenery and gather or make the props; some would take care of getting the costumes together and do makeup; others would write and send the invitations to the parents, staff, and other guests and also design and produce the program; and still others would take care of the curtain and give cues or prompt the actors.

The actors. I wanted so much to be one but was certain I could never expose myself in that manner. I couldn't be that open, that vulnerable to the class or to Mr. Seidman, let alone an audience of mostly strangers. Of course, I didn't volunteer for any of the parts. But deep inside I ached to act, to be a performer—and yes, to show myself off—because somehow and somewhere in that very same deep inside I guess I believed I could do it. And so did Mr. Seidman. He assigned me a part in the play with one of his lovely, generous smiles. He said I had no choice in the matter but to do a good job of it and he had no doubt that I would. I was to play another character's mother, and since the play was set at the turn of the century—don't ask me why—I would wear a long dress with a bustle and a great big hat with long feathers. We, the class, had written a lot of slapstick material into the play, and the role of this mother had many funny lines.

It *was* impossible for me not to do it, to say no to Mr. Seidman. It was a great part and if I did it right—*me*—I would get the chance to make people laugh. Is there anything better than being able to make people laugh? It was impossible to resist, not only because I really wanted to do it, but because Mr. Seidman convinced me that I could. He had me read a little of the play while he did all the other parts. During rehearsals, he encouraged me to speak up, to exaggerate my voice and gestures, to really ham it up. This was, after all, a comic character and I would provide a lot of the play's comic relief. Remember, this was a play about teeth and their care, which in real life would have to be about the pain and sorrow of decay and further probable pain incurred by visits to the dentist with drills and needles. Mr. Seidman kept saying I had it. What it took. I was going to be wonderful.

The first afternoon I got my script home, I immediately began memorizing my lines. I felt freer to try out more daring and outlandish gestures, facial expressions, and moves than I had at school. I rehearsed constantly every day, both at home and at school, fine-tuning my part. At home, Mami helped me learn my lines. She also made my costume, an old dress of hers with big shoulder pads. She had sewn in a small pillow in the back that was meant to be the bustle. She was so proud I had gotten this big part in the school play, her shy little Lidin. Every evening Mami held the script tightly, scanning each word carefully as I recited the words. When I faltered, she would mouth the word; if I still didn't get it, she would say it aloud with her unique accent and pronunciation, her love and pride helping me become more familiar and eventually comfortable with the words I was committed to learn. Mami had faith in me, just like Mr. Seidman. How could I not succeed?

The night of the performance I was so excited, nervous, and scared I thought I would throw up. Mr. Seidman came backstage and asked us all to form a circle, he himself becoming part of our circle. We held one another's hands and in his quiet, reassuring voice, he reminded us how hard and long we had worked for that special night. He knew we were going to be just great. He asked us to repeat those words: "We're going to be great." He put his hand high in the air and made a big V for victory before walking out to join the rest of our audience. My hands were so sweaty that the sides of my dress where I kept wiping them had wet marks. As the curtain started going up, I went blank. I couldn't remember a single word. In ten minutes it would be my turn to go on stage.

When the time came, I did go on. Feeling every inch like a wooden marionette, I stopped at dead center stage. Paralyzed with inaction, I looked out into the audience and then to my fellow actor, who waited, almost as panic-stricken as I, for my lines. If I didn't say them, what was he supposed to do? Luckily, my eyes finally came to rest on Mr. Seidman's kind, accepting face. He whispered the first three words of the disappeared dialogue and smiled. Then all the words came to me, all the words I had worked so hard on, the words that Mami and Mr. Seidman had helped me with for weeks. Someone giggled at the first line and that was all the approval I needed to continue. I relaxed myself into the very familiar, well-practiced gestures, the funny faces, double takes, the inflections I knew to give certain words to make them more powerfully comic. Walking back and forth across the stage, I addressed the other actors and exaggerated my actions. The motions made the bustle on my behind—the pillow Mami had sewn into her old dress —bounce up and down as if it were an independent entity and that, in turn, caused the audience to laugh even harder. I was making people other than my classmates or my teacher or Mami laugh. Getting applause.

At the end of the play we all came out for our bows, and among Mr. Seidman's many bravos to us all, I clearly heard him say, "Bravo, Lydia. Bravo, bravo." I looked all over the auditorium for Mami, and finally I found her there right in the middle of the others assembled. She was there wiping away her tears but with a great big grin on her face. And me? My crush for Mr. Seidman grew stronger each day, just as strong and constant as the faith he had had in me. I still have that crush on him.

& Mieko Kamii

My History Lesson

The Ulysses S. Grant School in Los Angeles was built as a sturdy, two-story brick grammar school with high ceilings, large windows, and polished wooden floors. In steady succession between 1913 and 1932, first my mother then her four brothers and one sister all attended Grant. And after a long gap, I followed family tradition and enrolled in kindergarten there in 1951. I was living with my grandparents at the time. Their two-bedroom bungalow was home to eight people —three generations. To our *haku-jin* (the Japanese term for Caucasian or white) neighbors who knew my mother only as a woman who cleaned houses and who sent her child to school in hand-me-down clothes each day, we must have seemed a hard-luck bunch. But it had not always been this way.

Grandpa Aiso and his brother had emigrated to California in 1895 from Shizuoka-ken ("ken" means prefecture, a geopolitical unit in Japan, like a state). My grandmother and her sister joined the Aiso brothers in Los Angeles in 1903 as "picture brides," knowing their prospective spouses only in photographs exchanged through a marriage broker who matched eligible men in the United States with women from their home prefectures in Japan. By the time my mother was old enough to enter public school, Grandpa's strawberry farm in Burbank had failed. So he moved his family to Hollywood, then an exclusive area of Los Angeles where very few Japanese lived but where the schools were good. Grandpa worked as a gardener, mowing lawns, tending flowers, and trimming hedges for haku-jin customers. He enrolled first my mother, then Uncle John in Grant. Grandpa was determined that his children, all U.S. citizens, would be educated. And as affirmation of his dream, he donated to the grammar school its first American flag. Over the years, as each of Grandpa's six sons and daughters enrolled at Grant, they saw Grandpa's gift waving from the school's flagpole.

My mother met my father, Yoshio Kamii, when she was a student at Hollywood High School. A recent immigrant from Japan, Yoshio had been attending a Methodist college in Japan when a Methodist family in Los Angeles offered to sponsor a Japanese student and cover his college tuition if the student would agree to become their houseboy. My father answered the family's call. He learned English, earned his undergraduate degree from the University of Southern California, and with much personal and financial difficulty, he earned an MBA from the Harvard Business School. Frustrated by the lack of opportunity for Japanese men in the United States, my father accepted an offer to join the Japanese delegation in the International Labor Organization, a branch of the League of Nations, in Geneva, Switzerland. He and my mother married and departed for Switzerland. Luckily the French classes she took in college gave her enough language proficiency to rent an apartment and establish a household abroad. My brother Arthur and sister Constance (Connie) were born in Geneva in comfortable circumstances. Because the Swiss government assigned the citizenship of the father, not the mother, to children born within its borders, Arthur and Connie became citizens of Japan—a country they had never seen.

In 1939, Japan withdrew from the League of Nations, leaving my father unemployed. Seeing little alternative, he moved the family to Tokyo, and my American mother became a foreigner once again. When war with the United States broke out in 1941, the Japanese government gave Mother the opportunity to leave the country—but only if she left her husband and children in Japan. So she stayed. Dad abhorred the militarist Japanese government and refused to work for it. He accepted a job instead with a branch of the British American Tobacco Company in China and spent World War II separated from the family, traveling back and forth between the company's offices in Shanghai and Beijing.

In March 1942 my mother's parents, Grandpa and Grandma Aiso, their three younger children, Mary, Dan, and Jim, and all people of Japanese ancestry living on the West Coast in the United States were incarcerated in inland concentration camps (known as Executive Order 9066). My relatives were sent to live behind barbed wire at Manzanar in the California desert, one of eight camps scattered in remote, godforsaken areas of the country. The large-scale evacuation was a result of wartime hysteria and the culmination of more than fifty years of racial prejudice against the Japanese. My family had its own stories of such prejudice. In 1923, Joseph LeConte Junior High opened as the second junior high in Los Angeles. Among the first class of ninth-graders at LeConte was my uncle John. He was elected LeConte's first student body president, winning some nine hundred of the twelve hundred votes cast by his schoolmates. But this provoked protests from some of the parents, who objected to having "a Jap" in such a leadership role. A local newspaper that shared this prejudice began a series of stories and editorials about trouble at the school. The beleaguered principal of LeConte was told that either he had to get rid of John as student body president or the aroused parents would get rid of him. In the end the opposing factions hammered out a compromise that solved their embarrassing problem: They abolished the student government for the year.

By the time the war broke out in 1941, John and his brother Paul had already received greetings from Uncle Sam and were serving as instructors in the Military Intelligence Service Language Schools. Their younger brothers, my Uncles Dan and Jim, spent a brief time at Manzanar and then, like so many young Nisei males in the concentration camps, they demonstrated their loyalty by enlisting in the armed forces. (Nisei, Japanese for "second generation," is the term used by Japanese Americans to refer to the children born in the United States to Japanese immigrants.) The four Aiso brothers were among the more than twenty-five thousand Japanese Americans who served in the armed forces during World War II. When the war ended in 1945, and General Douglas MacArthur's occupation forces needed staff who were fluent in Japanese, three of Mom's brothers—John, Dan, and Jim—were sent to Tokyo as victorious American soldiers. Uncle John assisted General Willoughby in prosecuting war criminals, Uncle Dan dispensed supplies, and Uncle Jim drove trucks. And general headquarters welcomed the assistance of my father, who had returned to Japan and was fluent in both Japanese and English.

When I was an infant, my older brother Arthur was stricken with polio. As we were still living in Japan, Mother was desperate to get Arthur to Los Angeles, where experimental procedures for treating the disease were being developed. She insisted that Dad seek permission to leave Japan. After all, she was an American citizen, her brothers were in the occupation forces, both Dad and Uncle John were attached to general headquarters, and her parents owned property in California. My father made persistent requests, and MacArthur finally decided it would be good for public relations to allow Arthur passage to America, as a humanitarian act. Mother accompanied him, because he was seventeen and spoke no English, and I accompanied Mother, because I was only fifteen months old. My older sister Connie arrived a year and a half later on a student visa. It was six years before my father was granted the visa to join us. During that time the Japanese government allowed him to send only thirty dollars per month out of the country. Mother had no health insurance and borrowed heavily from Uncle Paul to cover Arthur's medical expenses. We had to rely on Grandma and Grandpa to house and feed us. And that is why we all lived on Tamarind Avenue in my grandparents' two-bedroom bungalow.

$\mathcal{E}$

I remember kindergarten at Grant as an exciting place, even if no one could say my name right. I loved building with the big wooden blocks—long ones, short ones, and ones you could use to make arches. I worked at mastering the finger, hand, and arm movements that made our songs come alive. I relished making dinners for special guests in the sandbox and wearing dress-up clothes that transformed me into a princess. For me, wearing a smock in front of an easel, mixing tempera paints in recycled milk cartons, and leaving wide swatches of red, blue, yellow, orange, green, and purple on newsprint was almost magical. I have fond memories of chattering to Grandma about what I did that morning or afternoon as we walked home, hand-in-hand each day. I was in love with kindergarten and with school.

But in first grade my complicated history began to weigh on me. I was a child who had been read to from an early age.

I heard my favorite stories repeated over and over again until I had them committed to memory. I protested every time Grandma or Connie tried to skip over a page or shorten a sentence. I thought I was reading, and indeed I was in my own way. Unfortunately, I was learning to read Japanese, not English. When my first-grade teacher found me struggling to make sense of Dick and Jane's adventures with their dog Spot, she placed me in "Group 3," the group we all knew was for the slow kids, the dumb kids, the kids who could not read. Now I was one of them, and I felt stupid, humiliated, and ashamed.

First grade was not just reading, of course. Nineteen fifty-two was the presidential election year, Dwight Eisenhower against Adlai Stevenson. My teacher decided that holding a mock presidential election would be a valuable activity for her first-graders. She asked us to talk with our families about why voting was important and who they favored and why. My wisdom about presidents at the time was scanty. Washington and Lincoln peered down on our crowded household from re-production portraits that Grandpa had hung on the dining room wall, so they were familiar faces. But neither of them was running. With the exception of my father, who I knew only through the thin, blue, airmail sheets that arrived from Japan, ours was a thoroughly Republican family, so I knew how I was expected to vote.

Election day came at school and I was ready. When the moment arrived to cast our ballots, the teacher stopped me: "You can help me count the ballots. But you're not a citizen, so you cannot vote." Eisenhower won the presidential election that year by more than six million votes. He did not need the one vote of a disappointed, humiliated, perplexed six-year-old U.S.

citizen. My first-grade teacher had looked only at my Japanese face and had ignored my history. That was the year I was punished for aggressive behavior on the playground and sent to the principal's office for breaking school rules.

I have no notion how long I would have been tagged as a "Group 3" child at Grant if it had not been for Miss Koonz, my third-grade teacher. She was a small woman with weathered skin, stooped shoulders, and salt-and-pepper hair. She reminded me of Grandma even if Grandma's hair was all white. Miss Koonz was nearing retirement, having spent her entire career as a teacher at Grant. She had known all of Grandpa's children when they passed through Grant, and she knew our family's history. Miss Koonz understood why my parents had gone to Switzerland, Japan, and China, and why Uncle John's Harvard Law School degree wasn't enough to permit him to appear in U.S. courts. I was in her third-grade classroom for perhaps two months when she pulled me out one day to have me take some tests. I don't remember what they were, but after I finished, she told me that after Christmas I would be going to the fourth grade. She assured me I would make lots of new friends and enjoy the work.

When we returned after Christmas vacation, Miss Koonz walked me up the stairs to the fourth-grade classroom and introduced me to Miss Reed. It was just after lunch, and Miss Reed's students were seated on the floor, listening as she read *Charlotte's Web* aloud to them. Miss Reed smiled at me, asked me to find a place on the floor next to Gail Kusudo, the only other Japanese child at Grant, said Gail would help me get acquainted with the class, and then simply resumed reading. In short order I fell in love with the story, then with reading, and then once again, I fell in love with school.

I imagine that sometime during the years of war with Japan, the American flag that Grandpa Aiso had given to Grant became too faded and torn to fly over the school any longer. I wish I had asked Miss Koonz what became of the flag. She was good at remembering every child's history.

From Unbought and Unbossed

A blind political science professor, Louis Warsoff, became interested in me, and we had long talks. I called him "Proffy," affectionately. He was one of the first white men whom I ever really knew and trusted. Our white neighbors and my father's co-workers had never been friends; they did not visit us and we did not visit them, and our interrelations were always a little strained even when they were at their best. From Professor Warsoff I learned that white people were not really different from me. I loved formal debating particularly, and once after I starred in a match he told me, "You ought to go into politics." I was astonished at his naiveté.

S Lenore H. Gay

Mistresses of Magic

> *My imagination is a monastery*
> *and I am its monk.*
> ❧ John Keats

I dropped my head on my arms, closed my eyes, and waited for Miss Murray, my third-grade teacher, to adjust her glasses and open the book. My cot stood under the window and the sun shone through the window shade, warming my back. After a little cough, I heard pages turning. We were going to hear chapter five from *The Boxcar Children,* the story of four children, a family without grown-ups. As Miss Murray began to read, I left my cot and went with the boxcar children on their adventures. I headed for the dump to search for cups and spoons and other important stuff. We were orphans who found a home, an abandoned boxcar that sat on train tracks in the woods. We cooked our dinners outside over an open fire and slept inside the boxcar. Everything we found—berries, crooked nails, tree stumps, a pool of water, and old cups—we used. Ordinary things no longer had ordinary uses. We loved making do.

When nap time was over, I looked around to see if anyone else looked unusual, as if they'd left the room too. But all the girls were talking and laughing, as usual. I wondered if I was the only one. My parents had read to me since I was a baby, and I'd read to myself since I was three. But by the third grade my brother was the baby, and I was too old to hear stories at home. The best part of third grade for me was Miss Murray's stories.

Miss Murray was very old, with fuzzy white hair and black tie-up shoes. She was nice the first morning of school when we came in off the playground, and she stayed kind right through to our last day with her. Early in the year, she announced that the third grade would be the year to learn multiplication tables, all the way up to twelve times twelve. Wearing a gray crepe dress, with a matching fabric-covered belt, Miss Murray stood in front of the class explaining the idea of multiplying, which seemed confusing at first. But to my surprise, learning the tables was easy and fun. At home sometimes Daddy called them out to me: Six times seven? Six times eight? Sometimes I marched around the house, pretending to lead a parade of sticks that were shaped like numbers, shouting out the twos and threes, right on up through the twelves.

&

Things at my house were different than other houses. In fifth grade, when I began to spend the nights with girl friends in my class, I realized how different. No other girl's father was a painter; their fathers were doctors, or engineers, or lawyers. A few fathers didn't work but clipped coupons, which I imagined meant sitting at a desk with a pile of store coupons, trimming the jagged edges with a pair of scissors. No one else in my class had a father who painted nudes sprouting from giant flowers, or seven-legged animals roaming lavender hills, or tiny faces swirling up the trunk of a tree. My father ignored the yellow dye that came in the package of white margarine. Using food coloring, he dyed the margarine blue one week and red the next. Anything could happen.

I remember when a tiger got loose from the circus nearby. It hid in our willow tree. I had to catch him before he jumped down on our tent. My friend Sandy from across the street was hiding inside the tent under the blankets. I crawled out of the tent to climb the tree and instead ran into my house: "Can we have Cokes? What about calling the circus? The tiger's hungry. *National Geographic* says tigers eat at dark. It's dark and he's hungry."

Mother said, "Where's Sandy?"

"She's still in the tent and the tiger's gnawing on her right now. Tell her mother the tiger ate her daughter and we're sorry we didn't know camping was that dangerous." I inched down the back steps with two bottles of Coke, one under my chin, the other under my arm, bottle opener in my pocket. I pointed the flashlight at the willow tree. Looking for eyes. Orange, glowy eyes. I shined it everywhere. No stripes. No eyes. Sandy whispered, "Lenore, that you?"

"Yes, I got Cokes and Mother's going to phone. They'll come in a big truck with tigers and bears painted on the sides. Lots of men with a special tiger net. If they don't catch him by the time we drink our Cokes, Mother says it's okay to sleep inside."

I also used my imagination with the stars and moons Daddy had stuck all over my ceiling. At night I'd stare at them, blinking my eyes to make them jump around. I built a special car to take me and the moon elves all over the universe, like Sargeant Preston's horse Rex on the radio show. Rex took Sargeant Preston all over the Yukon. My imaginary friends Sir Robert, Margaret, and Lucinda lived in my head, and together we sailed around the moon, or jumped into the ocean and rode yellow catfish, which looked like tabby cats with scales. Every night I stared at those stars and the moon, wondering about things, until I fell off into a dream. When I was six and ran away, my make-believe friends came with me. I stuffed my pajamas, toothbrush, a Coke, and a *Teenie Weenies* book in a pillowcase.

It weighed too much to tie to a stick. Mother said I could run as far as her friend's house, and since that house was four blocks away, she watched me from the car.

⚓

But I couldn't use my imagination to make sense of math and grammar. My fourth-grade teacher wasn't nice like Miss Murray. I would stand at the blackboard, rocking from one foot to the other, with the teacher glaring at me as I struggled to make sense of a string of numbers. It was no better when the class diagrammed sentences. I'd pause, frozen, a piece of chalk in my hand, while the teacher wrote a sentence on the blackboard and told me to pull it apart and diagram it. I'd draw a bunch of lines and start to put any old word on them, watching her out of the corner of my eye. She'd tap her foot, and when she put her hands on her hips, I'd stop writing. She would call my bluff. I hated her. In my head, I could combine words to make wonderful sounds but could not understand why she thought fitting words in a chart would help us to make good sentences.

By sixth grade I knew that writing stories and poems was okay, but that literature and history were not the most important subjects in school. Mastering geometry, biology, Latin, and being able to diagram a sentence were vital. By eighth grade I was doing poorly. I barely passed geometry, repeating it in summer school. With some struggle I also completed a "dummy" math class. It was becoming clear to me that I was a dummy.

If not for Miss Salley, the drama coach, I might have finished high school believing in my stupidity. But she was a conjurer. She caused qualities and talents to appear from inside many girls, including me, as if by magic. She found my gift in my ability to make believe. A tiny, impish lady, Miss Salley had a voice that carried a trill and her high-spirited laugh could fill a room. Between the third and twelfth grades students performed several of Shakespeare's plays, and Miss Salley helped me to love his work. Even though she'd tap the stage with her wooden stick whenever anyone made a mistake, I wasn't afraid of her. In her presence I felt awe and the desire to please.

In an all-girls' school no part was off-limits; we played them all—elf, tramp, soldier, prince, and queen. In third grade I tried out for *The Tempest* and turned into old Gonzalo with an itchy, gray beard, feigning a dry death. Shakespeare meant lots of practice and memorizing, and I'd pace around the house shouting out my lines. Later, I played fair Hippolyta, swirling around in blue robes, hailing the arrival of my nuptial hour in *A Midsummer Night's Dream*. Hippolyta's opening line described the moon as "a silver bow new bent in heaven." For another role in *A Midsummer Night's Dream*, a fairy, I painted my legs gold. Miss Salley said to leave patches of skin unpainted because the skin needs to breathe. I told everyone I was risking full body poisoning. Being on stage might be worth an early death. Even when the parts were small, to feel included was enough.

In sixth grade I played Carol in *The Birds' Christmas Carol*, my favorite tearjerker. In the final scene, terminally ill, I coughed and coughed, languishing on a pink chaise longue, lying still while the stage dimmed and went black. Afterward, tearful classmates gathered around, wanting reassurance. Carol was only resting? Feeling triumphant, I said, "No, she died." They turned away, grim, like they'd lost a friend. Miss Salley said my voice was good and that I projected just right—coughing, expiring loudly enough for even the balcony's last row to hear.

Behind the theater stood the most exciting place in school, Miss Salley's Blue Room. The Blue Room was a wardrobe shed crammed full of costumes: racks of dresses, leotards, and fur coats, and lots of fairy skirts, pink and green tulle with silver flecks. Crowns with rhinestones and emeralds, wigs and hats piled high on shelves. For the male parts black wool pants, maroon smoking jackets, staves, top hats, and swords. Red officer coats trimmed in bumpy gold braid.

With each performance I forgot myself and turned into someone I'd never known, someone far different than the outsider at school I sometimes felt. And teachers who appreciated creativity helped me to feel welcome. With each story, with each play, Miss Salley and Miss Murray, the mistresses of magic, taught me that it was good to imagine. It's a lesson I haven't forgotten.

ぷ James Earl Jones

From Voices and Silences

For me, the pivotal teacher was Donald E. Crouch, a former college professor who came out of retirement to teach us English, Latin and history. I was still a mute when I entered high school. I had gotten through eight years of school without using the power of speech unless I was forced to.

The turning point in my ability to cope with my stuttering came in Professor Crouch's English classroom. He introduced me to good literature—Shakespeare, Emerson, Longfellow. Because it had taken place in our part of the country, I especially loved Longfellow's "Song of Hiawatha." In fact, I was so inspired that I started writing poetry, and poetry got me into trouble, and then, ironically, changed my life.

During the Depression and on into the war, the government shipped surplus food around the country, staples and perishables, any overabundance of fruits. We knew when the food train was coming to town, and we could get our welfare allotment of whatever the train was handing out on that trip. One winter, we got grapefruit, shipped all the way from Florida to Michigan on the food train. We hardly ever had grapefruit in our house.

The taste of it knocked me out, the pure, juicy luxury of grapefruit in winter. I decided to write a poem about it, patterned after the poem I knew best—Longfellow's "Song of Hiawatha." I forced my grapefruit rhapsody into Longfellow's cadence and rhyme scheme. Fortunately, no copy of that poem survives.

I was proud of my effort, however. Somehow Professor Crouch, to his surprise and pleasure, discovered that I wrote poetry. The boy who had written the poems was the same mute boy who had fought with uncontrolled fury. Both fury and poetry poured out of my silence.

"I'm impressed with your poem, James Earl," Professor Crouch told me after he read my ode to grapefruit. "I know how hard it is for you to talk, and I don't require you to do that. Unfortunately, it is hard for me to know whether these are your words. This is a fine poem. Did you copy it from somebody?"

My honor was at stake. Plagiarism was bad business. I had written every word of this poem myself. I would never copy someone else's poem and claim it for my own.

"I think the best way for you to demonstrate that you wrote this poem yourself is for you to say it aloud to the class," he told me.

It would be a trauma to open my mouth in front of classmates, who would probably laugh at my poem and my stuttering. But it would be a greater trauma to be disgraced, unfairly charged with plagiarism. Now I would just have to open my mouth in public in self-defense.

I was shaking as I stood up, cursing myself. I strained to get the words out, pushing from the bottom of my soul. I opened my mouth—and to my astonishment, the words flowed out smoothly, every one of them. There was no stutter. All of us were amazed, not so much by the poem as by the performance.

Professor Crouch and I had stumbled on a principle which speech therapists and psychologists understand. The written word is safe for the stutterer. The script is a sanctuary. I could read from the paper the words I had composed there, and speak as fluently as anybody in the class.

"Aha!" my professor exclaimed as I sat down, vindicated. "We will now use this as a way to recapture your ability to speak."

◈ Dorothy V. Smith

"Oh Freedom": Education in the Piney Woods of Mississippi

McComb, Mississippi, is a small city located eighty miles south of Jackson and one hundred miles north of New Orleans. It made national news, maybe even international news, during the civil rights movement as a tough town for Black people. I was born in McComb as the baby and only girl in a family of three children, later four when my parents adopted my baby brother. I grew up in poverty, unaware of my family's meager resources, but I never wanted for the necessities of life. I lived every day with racism, but excellent teachers like Ms. McLeod, Mr. Therrell, and Rev. Bingham, all of them Black, taught me that I could become whatever I wanted. They believed I was very bright. They pushed me and loved me into achievement.

The summer of my first year in junior high, I attended Freedom School in a Black church located next to a housing project. This was a new and exciting experience for me. I was introduced to foreign languages, photography, and Black history, subjects that had not been allowed in my regular school. I was taught by a young white male named Ira Landis. Ira, as he told us to call him, impressed me immediately. He was a kind and understanding teacher who gave me his undivided attention. He was the first white person to whom I had ever been close enough to touch, yet I did not feel uncomfortable when I was with him. I knew the schools I had attended were not as good as the white schools in McComb and certainly nothing like the schools in New York, where Ira had taught. The building I attended in elementary school had been a chicken-processing plant. My junior high school was okay, but it didn't have many of the materials our teachers wanted and needed. Ira made me feel that, despite what McComb had not given me, I was as sharp as the white students he had taught in New York—even smarter than many of them. What I did not know he attributed to lack of exposure, not to lack of intelligence.

During Christmas break, students in every Freedom School in McComb were treated to a trip to New York to hear Malcolm X, whom we had learned about in our classes. For me the trip was a big treat because I had never traveled outside the South. When I boarded the chartered bus with other students, with civil rights workers, and with Freedom School teachers, I carried an old brown tin loaded with my best attire and a shoebox filled with food. The trip took four-and-a-half days. We sang freedom songs all the way.

Harlem was unbelievable to me. Blacks were everywhere, and they were moving at what I considered a rapid pace. Malcolm was inspiring to me. He delivered a speech that would later be published in *Malcolm X Speaks* as "Address to the Youth of McComb, Mississippi." Freedom School, Ira, the trip to New York, and the lecture by Malcolm X changed my life. When I returned to regular school at the end of the summer, I was more determined than ever to become a teacher of Black history. Today, as I prepare lectures for my history classes at Dillard University, I often journey in memory to my regular school and to Freedom School, each time saying thanks to Ira, to Ms. McLeod, Mr. Therrell, and Rev. Bingham for helping me become what I wanted to become.

↤ James Knudsen

Gifts: Four Teachers, Four Stories

The teachers we remember most fondly are often the teachers who saw something remarkable in us. These teachers
looked as hard as they had to and nurtured what they found. In
the final analysis all students have gifts to bring their teachers
(however small they may sometimes seem to be), and the most
successful teachers, and probably the happiest, are those with
the ability and tenaciousness to find the most gifts among their
students. Just as teachers find gifts in their students, their students take gifts from them. Intangible things like knowledge,
confidence, and skill. Teachers often don't know what gifts
their students are taking. It may be the material outlined in the
course plan or syllabus, but instead of this material, students
frequently take something else: the quiet girl in the back row
who goes on to read the rest of Hemingway's work the summer
after graduation because she was inspired by a teacher's assignment of "A Clean, Well Lighted Place," or the boy who pur-
sues the study of genetics years after a seed was planted in
sophomore biology.

We live in a culture that loves winners. For example, we're
not content to isolate the top five performances in any of the
acting categories at the Academy Awards; we want one to be
singled out as the only winner. The same is true of teaching
awards. When you ask people to name their favorite teacher,
most try to isolate a single one. They study their memories
looking for a teacher who changed their lives, a teacher who led
them to their major in college or selected them for the cheer-

leading squad or the debate team. I suspect, though, that for most of us, many teachers have made significant contributions, and whether any one could be named the best really isn't important. Teachers don't have to be magnificent at all aspects of the job to make a profound difference in the lives of their students. Their gifts come in all sorts of packages.

When I was in high school during the mid- to late 1960s, I had four remarkable English teachers who took it upon themselves to teach me what they loved and what gave them solace. During those four years I found the path and the passions that have since guided my life.

THE BLUE BIRD

Mrs. Parr was a marvelously energetic and theatrical woman no taller than five feet with a hairdo I'd seen in movies from the 1940s: large tortoiseshell combs held poufs of brassy hair behind her ears. As she talked, she would rearrange the combs. As she talked, she would lace her thumbs beneath the Civil War buckle that had been passed down to her from her great-grandfather. She never stopped talking. She talked about the books she loved, movies she wanted us to see, her family history.

Mrs. Parr's greatest gift to me was passing down her love of owning books. I probably always read more than the average kid, but 95 percent of my reading came from the town library's shelves and had to be returned within two weeks. As a child, I'd been given a few Golden Books, and then in fifth or sixth grade I'd bought several Hardy Boys adventures because the library deemed them too trashy to carry. In freshman English, Mrs. Parr amazed me with tales of her house, where floor-to-ceiling bookcases lined every room. She frequently brought books from home to show us. Occasionally the books were related to something we were discussing in class, but frequently they were just books she liked and wanted to recommend, such as *The Annotated Alice: Alice's Adventures in Wonderland and Through the Looking Glass* or the Tolkien trilogy. Each book she slipped from her leather satchel was sheathed in a homemade jacket of pink shelf paper with its title written in blue ink along the spine. She told us that she had similar jackets on every book in her vast collection, and I marveled at the thought of walls and walls of pink books, of Mrs. Parr seated at her kitchen table meticulously fitting them with their jackets.

In the spring of my freshman year, she began the drumbeat for a used-book sale to be held in a nearby town one Saturday. She described the wonders of the sale—books of all kinds, some priced as low as a dime, the sidewalk of half a city block jammed with overflowing card tables. She was planning to go and frequently mentioned that she would be looking for a copy of a book she'd been searching for for years, Maurice Maeterlinck's *The Blue Bird.* On the day of the event I couldn't scare up a fellow classmate who wanted to go, and my parents were too busy to drive me, so I ended up riding my balloon-tire bike several miles. By the time I arrived at the card tables, my heart was beating wildly—a combination, I suppose, of the exhausting ride and the excitement over finally seeing the tables of books that Mrs. Parr's words had been conjuring up in my mind for weeks.

I immediately went to work scanning the titles, and while I was poking through a large box under one of the tables, after gleefully combing through all the books on top, I found a thin navy blue volume with gold lettering on the cover. Although it was old, it seemed to be in excellent condition. I could hardly believe my eyes when I deciphered the gothic letters: *The Blue Bird* by Maurice Maeterlinck. With trembling hands I opened the cover. It was fifteen cents. I think I passed out for an instant. Not only had I found the book that Mrs. Parr had talked about all spring, but I had enough money to actually buy it and bring it to her. It didn't matter if I found another book, but I kept looking anyway, out of some vague sense that I was on a roll.

A short time later I noticed a small woman approaching the sale tables from down the street. I could see the poufs of hair poking out from under a pink scarf. "Mrs. Parr," I called out as I ran toward her. "I found it!" She was nearly speechless with gratitude, and neither of us could stop talking about the incredible irony of it all. That night I imagined her lovingly cutting and folding a pink jacket for *The Blue Bird* before sliding it on her shelf. I emptied my own new bag of books and found a place for them on the empty shelf next to the Hardy Boys. No book covers for me. From that day on I've rarely missed a used-book sale. I've always traveled with my own wish list and every now and then have turned up my own "blue birds." Mrs. Parr passed on to me the pleasure of book ownership and the fun of sifting through used books looking for treasure. I can just imagine her delight walking through my house today, seeing my own floor-to-ceiling bookshelves.

SEMANTICS: THE MAGIC OF WORDS

Mr. Hible, my English teacher junior year, treated me and the other students like world-weary adults, the world-weary adults that at sixteen we thought we were. He seemed to realize that we were a class full of budding Holden Caufields; he made just the right bleak jokes to endear himself. I remember a slight man who wore dark suits, white shirts, and dark ties, the horn-rimmed glasses of a young businessman of the 1960s. He had four children and often began class with a dark tidbit from home. One night, for instance, his innocent daughter had begun to sing "I'm a little teapot, short and stout" and then had added a contemporary twist: "Sock it to me baby, let it all hang out." At times, Mr. Hible's bleak humor devolved into pure bleakness. There was an adult despair I realize now that we couldn't comprehend. He spent his weekends working on a screenplay with a faculty member from the Sociology Department. It was to be an exposé of the hollowness of suburban life filmed entirely at a discount center called E. J. Korvette's.

I will always be grateful to Mr. Hible for expanding my vocabulary, my love of words as entertainment. He was the man who assigned me Sidney J. Shanker's *Semantics: The Magic of Words*. He was the man who added a weekly word to Shanker's vocabulary lists (lists we were required to study as part of the state curriculum in Illinois). These weren't just any words but words Mr. Hible had selected for their appeal to our premature jadedness: licentious, salacious, rapacious. He always introduced these words with a wicked laugh. I don't specifically remember any of the other words I learned that year, but I'll always remember those three. He taught me to love unusual words, to store them like treasures: They could be suggestive, weird, and just plain useful. My classmates and I teased each other about having salacious smiles and rapacious appetites. We dropped Mr. Hible's words into our conversations, where they remain to this day.

L'ETRANGER

Miss Bush had been a WAC (a member of the Women's Army Corps) during World War II and had a certain military air about her, from her boxy shoes and crisp gait to the way she combed her graying brown hair into a short ducktail and wore fitted blazers over khaki skirts. There were surprises too: the intense red lipstick and the string ties with rhinestone slides. As controlled and disciplined as she was at most times, she would occasionally succumb to outbursts of anger. We were cocky seniors. We asked why too often in regard to her assignments. One time we were quite sure we even made her cry with our petition asking that we not have to read our book reports out loud anymore.

Miss Bush never missed an opportunity to tell us it was dark out there in the world. She'd seen war firsthand and evil in the city that she warned would one day absorb our tiny suburb. She whispered in our ears that things just might not turn out the way we planned. She let us know that life had its own ideas— sometimes we'd just be hanging on. If you feel like you're in control, just wait! If we'd thought we were jaded in Mr. Hible's class, with Miss Bush we discovered we'd barely explored the meaning of the word.

Under her direction we read great existential works: *No Exit* and *The Stranger* (which she, in a voice that was oddly threatening, always referred to as *L'Etranger*). For our final project of the year she assigned us to create collages or Super 8 movies or poems that would express who we were, circa the late 1960s. When she saw the rainbow wash of my collage, with its central figure, a young man, pulling the sun from the sky, Miss Bush must have laughed darkly to herself about the price I would one day pay for such innocence. I must have created it as a talisman against the dark world I'd already begun to glimpse outside of school thanks to Miss Bush's course plans.

From Miss Bush I received my introduction to the big picture, to what Flannery O'Connor once called "the world of guilt and sorrow." Some people, I suppose, might not think of this as a gift, but it was a valuable lesson for me. Later, when I began to experience the full range of sadness life can offer, I wasn't the naif I could've been. Miss Bush had already meddled with my innocence and given me a useful way of thinking about my losses.

"THE PUMPKIN TIDE"

Mrs. Gannon, with her crown of white hair and wardrobe of flowered caftans, was a supporter of writing in every way. She was the first English teacher I ever had who actually mentioned her own writing. The idea of a writer teaching writing—what a concept! More than any other teacher in that period in my life, Mrs. Gannon was the one who saw a gift in me. She had a habit in our creative writing class of reading aloud one or two responses to each assignment without identifying the writer. She would lavish praise on the pieces she read, but only she and the writer knew who was responsible for the work. More than a few times I sat in class, glowing inside as she read my latest work to the unsuspecting class. How I clung to that praise. I said to myself, "I'm a writer. Mrs. Gannon believes I can do it." I began to believe it too.

Mrs. Gannon crammed her classroom with the printed word. I remember a table at the back where I first encountered the *New York Times Book Review*. She set aside part of a class period every week for us to simply explore the reading material she'd collected. We could bring our own books or magazines as long as they weren't things we were reading for another class. Although she tried to encourage us to expand our horizons, she let the final choice of what to read be ours. I remember one student reading a custom car magazine and another a fan club newsletter devoted to Elvis. Allowing us to read what we chose gave us a clear sign that she respected our individuality, and at this point in my life I see it also revealed that teaching for her was an occupation built on hope: The student reading descriptions of Graceland's many rooms one day might eventually read her way to the rooms of Gatsby's mansion.

When I had gone off to college and had had my first poem accepted by a literary magazine at age nineteen, Mrs. Gannon was the one teacher from my high school with whom I shared the news. That spring semester break I returned to see her, and she gave me the heady experience of inviting me into the teacher's lounge for coffee. While there she pulled from her briefcase a poem by her latest discovery, her latest *me*. I immediately recognized that the poem, "The Pumpkin Tide," had been plagiarized from Richard Brautigan, a writer whose work I was just discovering myself. I told her who'd actually written the poem and watched her deflate with disappointment. I was almost sorry that I hadn't kept the truth to myself.

This experience unsettled me—could I possibly know something about writing that a teacher didn't know? Might it be possible for me to surpass Mrs. Gannon? I learned something about the fallibility of teachers that afternoon, but in the end it was her passion for her students' work that I took from her. She hadn't detected a case of plagiarism; she'd simply found a poem she loved and had thanked and praised the wrong poet. Her passion for writing, for my work, her gifts to me, fueled me through the early years of my apprenticeship as a writer.

&

Looking back at my life, I can see how things that happened even before I was in high school put me on the path toward becoming a writer and a teacher myself. Mrs. Hanson, my eighth-grade English teacher, wrote across the top of my book report on *The Red Badge of Courage,* "This is how writers begin." The idea that a writer begins as a lover of the work of other writers, as one who deeply appreciates their craft and vision, was too sophisticated for me to comprehend at the time, but Mrs. Hanson's words stuck with me until I was old enough to understand them. It was my high school English teachers, in their individual ways, who inspired me and gave me the confidence to believe I could do it. They weren't just teachers in the classroom sense; they modeled a lifestyle, where words and books were important, where noticing details and looking beyond the surface were required, where the life of the mind was a passionate thing.

✑ Arthur J. Clement
Remembering Mo Hunt

I spent the last two years of high school attending Deerfield Academy, a New England boarding school in western Massachusetts. For a Black boy living during the 1960s, this was both a great opportunity and a devastating loss. But Moreau Cosby Hunt helped me survive that experience and redeem it. "Mo Hunt," as he was affectionately called, was my English teacher and track coach. I struggled academically at Deerfield for the first time in my life. My sense of myself was shaken; I felt like a fish out of water. But Mo Hunt stood by me on many important occasions. I only discovered how important those moments were when I reconnected with him after three decades.

During the spring term in Mo Hunt's English IV class, I chose to write a term paper on three African-American novels: Richard Wright's *Native Son*, Ralph Ellison's *Invisible Man*, and James Baldwin's *The Fire Next Time*. These novels spoke to my condition as a Black student living at a white prep school. I needed to sort through my own jumbled feelings about race. Mo Hunt did not object to my selections, although he was unfamiliar with these writers. I completed the term paper and received my highest grade in his class. The paper is still in my possession today. Only later would I fully comprehend the extent to which Mo Hunt understood my yearnings as a fractured adolescent boy.

Coming back to Deerfield as a trustee after graduating thirty years before, I confronted my deeply ambivalent feelings. The appointment to the Board of Trustees was more than an honor; it was an opportunity for me to heal the pain of disconnection and self-doubt that I had experienced as a student there. Visiting the campus several times a year, attending meetings and classes, talking with faculty and students, I became an involved trustee and active alumnus. When Deerfield began its bicentennial celebration in 1997, I was asked to speak during a homecoming weekend hosted by the English Department. I knew that I must speak about my relationship with Mo Hunt, and the successes he had overseen as my teacher and coach. By now he had retired and was living in Vermont. I sent him track pictures from several newspaper clippings and told him about my upcoming talk. Mo Hunt dictated his response to his wife, Kitty:

> I remember you well and I also remember the wonderful afternoons at the track. . . . Thank you so much for the track pictures. I am sorry to be so late in responding to your very nice letter, but I have Parkinson's and it has slowed my mental and physical abilities considerably. . . . It's great to know that my English class and the books that you read have meant so much to you. Teaching meant so much to me. I'd love to still be teaching. I am so sorry those days are over.

My talk, "The Teacher Is Father to the Child," became a tribute to Mo Hunt and his gentle presence during our classes together, writing, rewriting, and discussing my final term paper at Deerfield. Following my talk, a member of the English faculty, John O'Brien, explored the Wordsworth poem "The Child Is Father to the Man" and drew connections between my literary allusion, Mo Hunt, and how English instruction was practiced at Deerfield. I was quite surprised to hear John tell the audience,

I'll let you in on a little secret. We teachers do this job not so much because we love to teach, but because we love to learn. And that love, if we're unstinting in our sharing of it, becomes our students' love, your love. I'll bet everyone here a nickel that Mo Hunt introduced Art Clement to Ralph Ellison, not so that he could instruct Art all about African-American writers. Rather, I wager, Mo did it to find out what he could learn about African-American writers from Art. And if Art indeed "grasped his identity" as his teacher hoped he might, you can be sure that Mo's identity as a teacher was enhanced as well.*

After the homecoming weekend, I sent a copy of my talk to Mo Hunt and Kitty. He responded by dictating these words: "I can't begin to tell you how much your talk meant to me, to Kitty, and to all our family. I'm sorry my poor health kept me away. I would have given anything to have been there. Right now I don't feel well enough to make my thoughts clear. But you have given me a wonderful feeling that will help me through some of my worst days."

Later that year Mo Hunt passed away. I was saddened when I heard the news, but I was satisfied knowing we had closed the loop.

---

*Janet W. B. Rodgers and Eric Widmer, *The Transcendent Mirror: A Bicentennial Anthology for Deerfield* (Deerfield, Mass.: Deerfield Press, 1999), 73.

✂ Joyce King
A Teacher's Touch

M any of us have heard testimonies about teachers who can "see" into a student's future. Even if a student is not performing well, they can predict success. We are convinced that this ability, this gift, is evidence that they were "called to teach." If the gift of sight is evidence, how greater must be the gift of touch. I have a testimony.

I grew up in the fifties in a poor African American neighborhood in Stockton, California, that had neither sidewalks nor an elementary school. Each day, always in groups at our parents' insistence, my friends and I would leave home early enough to walk eight blocks to school and be in our seats when the bell rang. We were not "bussed" to school. We walked. For four blocks, we walked on dusty roads. By the fifth block, we walked on sidewalks that led to lovely homes and to Fair Oaks Elementary School. It was at Fair Oaks, in a sixth grade English class, that I met Ms. Victoria Hunter, a teacher who had a profound effect on my life.

During silent periods, she would walk around the room, stop at our desks, stand over us for a second or two, and then touch us. Without saying anything to us (nothing could break the silence of reading periods), she would place two fingers lightly on our throats and hold them there for seconds. I learned many years later when I was a student at Stanford University that teachers touch the throat of students to check for sub-vocalization, which slows down the reading speed. I did not know at the time why Ms. Hunter was touching our throats, but I was a serious and respectful student and so, during silent reading period, I did what Ms. Hunter told us to do. I kept my eyes on the material I was reading and waited for her to place her fingers lightly on my throat.

One day, out of curiosity (perhaps there was another reason), I raised my head from my book—though not high—so that I could see Ms. Hunter, a white woman from Canada, moving up and down the rows, stopping at the desks of my peers. I wanted to see how they reacted when she touched their throats. She walked past them. I was confused. Did she pass them by because they were model students? What did we, the students who were touched, not do right? I sat up straighter in my chair, thinking that slumping in my seat might be the problem. I was confused. Several days later, I watched again, this time raising my head a little higher. Nothing had changed. Ms. Hunter touched the same students. Always, she touched me.

She touched me with her hands. She also touched me with her belief in my ability to achieve. She motivated me by demanding the best from me and by letting teachers I would meet in junior high school know I was coming, that I should be challenged, that I would be serious about my work. I am convinced that she touched me because she could "see" me in the future. That was true of all of us at Fair Oaks who sat still and silent as Ms. Hunter placed her fingers lightly on our throats. We left Fair Oaks as "best students," entered college-prep classes at John Marshall Junior High School, finished at the top of our high school class, and went on to earn graduate degrees in various disciplines. Ms. Hunter saw us achieving and she touched us to make certain that we would.

I was not surprised that she came to my graduation ceremony at Edison High School in Stockton or that she talked to me about finishing college and earning a Ph.D. She expected that of me. She gave me a beautifully wrapped box. Inside was a gift that adorns even as it touches me: a bracelet to which I can add charms for each stage of my life.

⚘ ⚘ ⚘ TWO

Respect and Passion for the Discipline

Teaching is the toughest and most important job in America.
⚘ Charles Dutton,
award-winning actor, director, and producer

❧ From a Conversation
with Jill Ker Conway

Teaching is a moral and sacred act. I think the characteristics of a good teacher begin with genuine respect for the student's mind. That respect conveys to students that they can take themselves seriously. Next to that, I think, is a real love for the young and joy in seeing them grow and develop. Next to that is a passion for the discipline. You can be passionate about your discipline, but if you lack respect for the young mind and the love of young people, you won't be able to communicate it very well.

We can teach people how to be good teachers up to a relatively high degree, but I think teaching is also a talent. The really great teachers have this kind of X-ray vision that allows them to look at a young person and see right into that important intersection of emotion and intellect and see how to harness that emotional energy and intellectual effort and bring it to fruition. And that is a kind of X-ray vision that can't be taught. You either have it or you don't.

‽ Anita Farber-Robertson

Mrs. Lewis, a Tribute

S he pushed her chair back from the big old wooden desk and stood, slightly wobbly in her high heels. The room quieted. All eyes watched. Walking to the blackboard, she found her balance and the wobble steadied. Still, she had to stand on tiptoes to reach the upper section of the board as she stretched out her arm and began writing in big clear letters "AIM." It was the first day of school.

Below the bold heading, a long sentence (or maybe it was a short paragraph) peeled off her fingertips onto the board. I do not remember what it said. I do remember being startled and confused. I was just barely nine years old. With that introduction Class 4–1 met Mrs. Lewis, who would be our fourth-grade teacher for the year. It was going to be different from the other classrooms we had known at P.S. 98 in Manhattan. That was obvious. Every class lesson Mrs. Lewis began the same way. She turned and wrote in sweeping strokes on the board "AIM," followed by a colon with a sentence or two explaining what would be the goal or purpose of the lesson in which we were about to engage.

I accepted this new routine quickly. Only now in the remembering does it have the power to bring tears to my eyes. How amazing to have a teacher who so respected nine-year-olds as to tell them, each day, each lesson, why they were doing the work she laid before them. How filled with love and honor was this teacher who revealed what she was hoping we would learn from the time we shared together. With that open vulnerability, a tone was set, the place was safe and risk was possible. By enlisting us as collaborators and coconspirators in learning, Mrs. Lewis instilled self-esteem and an internalized respect for our own minds and our agency. It was an effective enlistment, because we lived it in her classroom every day. The act of writing the lesson's aim on the board was not technique. It was born of deeper values. That invitation to partnership in the learning/teaching process is but one example of the characteristic way in which she interacted with us. Like a window, it revealed the frame through which Mrs. Lewis saw us and then crafted the role she would play in our unfolding. I felt empowered and accountable.

Mrs. Lewis was not a soft touch. Her expectations were high. The class work was demanding, but it felt fair. She was demanding of us all, herself included, and everything that she demanded was within our power to achieve. Feeling honored by her trust and grateful for the privileges she extended, I was motivated to prove her right. What a shocking contrast this was to my experience the year before in third grade. In Class 3–1 Mrs. Ettlinger had a system. The first row, which was the row to her far left, was the "good row." The sixth row, which was the one to her far right, was the "bad row." If you did well on a test, you moved up a row. If you did poorly, you moved back a row. Behaviors in class, academic and otherwise, were rewarded and punished through seat assignments.

Every morning Mrs. Ettlinger inspected us for polished shoes, neatly combed and pulled back hair, clean fingernails, and freshly ironed handkerchiefs. We were eight years old. I almost always failed inspection. My mother did not get up and comb my hair in the morning; I struggled with it myself. My mother did not give me clean and freshly ironed handkerchiefs each morning. My mother did not polish my shoes each night and leave them gleaming for me to slip into in the morning. And at eight years old I was not allowed to iron hankies or polish shoes by myself. So each morning I failed inspection and, as a consequence, each morning I was reassigned a seat in a "worse" row from the one I had occupied the day before.

Eventually it became clear to me that no matter how hard I tried at the things about which I could do something—how diligent I was at the things under my control, how many excellent papers I handed in—I would always slide into being identified with badness. The advance in row assignment I made because of an excellent test grade would be wiped out the next morning for lack of a fresh hanky. If my shoes weren't shiny, I might move back two rows, having barely tasted the sweetness of advancement for an hour or two in the afternoon. So I reconciled myself to third grade in the sixth row.

I had a ball. The sixth row was populated with boys, many older than I was, who had been expelled from the local Catholic school as behavior problems. I didn't learn much academic material that year (as a result my penmanship is atrocious), but I did learn that I could enjoy mixing with students from a different culture than my own. I found those boys to have human hearts under their third-grade tough bravado. Still, except for learning to make the best of a bad situation, it was a year of living under punishment for things outside of my control. I learned that my response to such insidious and pervasive disempowerment, once the initial fight proved futile, was to disengage and create my own little world of small and private pleasures. The sixth-row boys and I laughed a lot.

Mrs. Lewis, in dramatic contrast, cultivated her students' development of an internal authority. She avoided telling us to do things because she said so. She expected that we would want to know why we were doing them, and she did her best to achieve that. For example, she expected us to learn history, as did the other teachers we'd known. And startlingly, she expected that we would know why we were learning it. As the fourth-grade teacher, she also had the unenviable task of teaching us long division. I remember that it was a challenge, and I remember embracing that challenge with excitement. I do not recall what she told us about why long division was important, but because of Mrs. Lewis, I believed that it would be well worth my while to learn it and learn it well. I was surprised by the laments and complaints expressed by my peers in other fourth-grade classes as the curse of long division lay upon them. If I am creating the impression that we were an "easy" class, mindless in our devotion and discipleship, I apologize to you, the reader, and to my classmates of P.S. 98's Class 4–1. We were not. There were occasional uprisings and protestations of defiance or resistance. One in particular comes to mind.

Fourth-grade curriculum in New York City, as I think is true in many locations, includes a local social studies focus, geography, history, current affairs, and so on. As New Yorkers, when we learned in social studies that New York was the fashion capital of the world, we believed it. When we learned that New York was the publishing capital of the world, we believed it. When we learned that New York was the financial capital of the world, we nodded sagely. We thought it right and logical that New York should be the home of the United Nations. And of course we knew that New York had the tallest building in the world, the Empire State Building. We let Mrs. Lewis whip right through those lessons. It seemed we were galloping along, at least sauntering at a nice speed, when we cruised into the next chapter.

Lulled into complacency, we were unprepared for what was about to disturb our sense of identity and geosocial location, bringing us to an abrupt halt. You see, we had moved from the study of New York City to the study of New York state.

We learned that Albany was the capital of the state. We squirmed a little. That didn't seem right. It didn't make sense. It didn't seem fair, but we went along with it. Mrs. Lewis was convincing. Besides, we had already learned that New York City was once the nation's capital before it was moved to Washington, D.C. Although as a class we thought they'd made a terrible mistake with that decision, some of us thought privately that it was probably just as well. The traffic in New York was already a horrific problem. Adding the state and federal governments to the mix would have made it unbearable. So we adjusted to the fact that Albany served as the state capital.

From there we went on, having regained our composure. We turned the page in our textbook. What we beheld was shocking. Staring at us in black and white was an incredible statement: "New York is a dairy state." Now we were sure that in this city of eight million people there was not one cow. None of us had ever seen a cow, except in cartoons or picture books. We tittered. We smirked conspiratorially behind lifted hands that covered our scornful, laughing faces. This was ridiculous. The joke reached its conclusion and we were ready to deal it its death blow. Raising our hands, speaking in earnest when called on, we expressed our protest. The book, we suggested, was old. It was out of date. Maybe New York was once a dairy state. It wasn't now. We were certain. But Mrs. Lewis stood her ground.

"How could New York be a dairy state when most of its population lived in our fair city, and there was not a cow within its

bounds?" we demanded. We went on as though we were trying a case before the Supreme Court. There were no cows in
Central Park, neither were there any in our local Inwood Park.
There was a farmhouse museum in Inwood, our neighborhood. It was a Dutch-style farmhouse furnished in the period
of two hundred years ago and had a docent who would take you
around and explain how there used to be farms where all of our
rent-controlled apartments now stood. "Used to be," we insisted with emphasis. Past tense.

Mrs. Lewis was patient if somewhat amused. She let us blow
off steam. She would not give us an inch. The textbook was not
that old, and, yes, there were dairy farms in most of New York
state. She was sure of it. We just shook our heads and didn't
know what to make of it. I don't think Mrs. Lewis insisted that
we believe her. She allowed us to continue to try to validate our
position, but she was clear and firm. She was convinced New
York was still a dairy state and that that was just one more thing
we were going to have to cope with—along with the state capital being in Albany. Through that whole unit I tried to imagine
the majestic statehouse, built with large blocks of imposing
granite, set in the midst of a velvet green lawn and surrounded
by fancy iron fences that contained dairy cows leisurely nib-
bling on the governmental grass. It was hard to believe, but
stranger things than that were true.

Mrs. Lewis did something else that embodied her profound
respect for us as wise and thinking persons despite our youth.
By midyear she had lined up a rotation. When the school year
concluded, every one of the nearly thirty of us would have had
the chance to teach one or two lessons to the class ourselves.
These were not faux lessons for practice or show. These were
real lessons in the curriculum that the class would be responsi-

ble for having learned. And each one of us got to be the teacher. I remember the wide range of intense and wonderful feelings that filled and lifted me on the week when it was my turn. It was a time of excitement and anxiety, of ego-building self-importance and humble terror. It was an opportunity to be the big shot, to be in charge. And it was a moment of awesome responsibility. Everyone would be counting on me to be prepared, to know my material, to be their teacher. And Mrs. Lewis would be sitting somewhere in the back of the room. I don't think she sat there as a critic. I do not recall us getting grades on our performance as teachers. But I do remember that I did not want to disappoint her.

A few days before it was my turn to teach, Mrs. Lewis handed over to me the sacred text. I felt my hands tremble as I lifted up the *Teacher's Manual,* the book that taught the teachers, the book that told them what they were to do, what was expected, what was required. I had never in my life had the chance to look at such a manual, let alone read it, handle it, use it as though it were written to help me. What had been secret was now open. The teacher was not a magician or a holy person with a special connection to the sacred and all powerful. Rather, she was a person with tools that helped her do her work in ways that would succeed. And this incredible person did not hog all of that for herself. She did not keep that special knowledge as privileged information so that she might hold the power of the gate, doling out the goodies as she saw fit. She flung the gates open, so that all who wanted might come and enter. Mrs. Lewis let us in. She let us have that manual. She let us know what she had known. She let us into the inner circle, invited us into the special society of those who could teach. We were, as I said, nine years old.

Opening that book, I stared into the beginning page of my assigned lesson. There at the top of the page, written out for the teacher's guidance and assistance was the goal of the lesson. "AIM" the book's page had written at the top. And I recognized in that amazing moment that Mrs. Lewis had betrayed her station, her class, her caste. I did not know the language, but I sensed the meaning of what she had done. The aim was something written for the guide and help of teachers. It was part of their privilege. Mrs. Lewis had thrown open the doors, knocked down the boundaries and the barriers between learners and teachers. She let us in and let us own our learning.

There was a lesson in Mrs. Lewis's behavior that even she may have been unable to articulate, and that I only grasped years later. It was a lesson of relinquishment. I observed and lived in a classroom for a year with an unassuming and dedicated teacher who embraced a theology of universalism. She never said it but she lived it, and we watched and flourished. Mrs. Lewis believed that every person, regardless of their gender, age, or station, was valuable, precious, worthy of respect and education. And that passionate belief led her to practice a theology of relinquishment. It is a lesson that those of us with privilege struggle to learn and to accept in our various walks of life. It is one that often strikes terror in our hearts. If we give up whatever it is that makes us special—age, knowledge, credentials, money, race—will we still be special in the universe —will we still be the beloved of God? To the extent that we waver, that our answer is a qualified yes, it is hard for us to relinquish our outer trappings of privilege.

In the presence of Mrs. Lewis I learned the paradoxical truth that those who are the most powerful, the most influential, are those who generously give their power away. She was functioning as a grassroots organizer, teaching nine-year-olds how to be effective leaders and teachers. She was a subversive in the most beautiful and powerful meaning of the word, using the espoused values of the culture to change it for the better. If that were all that Mrs. Lewis did, it would be enough. That was a lot. But I have another memory of her that also was transforming.

One day she announced in class that if we were really good and got through all of our scheduled work ahead of time (which that day it looked like we just might do), she would teach us choral speaking. Now I have never heard of any child, fourth-grader or otherwise, who jumped up and down with excitement at the prospect of choral speaking. But the way Mrs. Lewis presented it, we were intrigued. She had our attention.

The class was divided into three groups of voices: boys, girls, and mixed. During the course of the year we were allowed to switch groups if we wished. Most of us didn't, having bonded with our group and the parts we had learned. As the year progressed, Mrs. Lewis taught us poetry (among this repertoire were pieces by Robert Frost and Ogden Nash, the two poets I remember nearly fifty years later), which we would then recite in this speaking chorus. Unlike singing, none of us had to worry about being off key or out of tune. We each had parts we loved to recite and repeat, some of which we memorized over time. It was great fun. I do not think we ever performed any of that choral speaking in public.

We learned to self-validate. We did not need parents or other classes or the principal to tell us it was fine and good, that we were becoming impressive public speakers of poetry. Without an audience in wait, we only needed to validate ourselves. The performance became its own reward. That was another gift of Mrs. Lewis: Doing it was its own reward. And the reward was made sweeter by the literary treasures we were learning. We discussed the poetry, why Mrs. Lewis, as our director, wanted it spoken a certain way. I think sometimes we disagreed and had to argue it to resolution. She was the choral conductor, that we knew. It was not chaos in our class. But she led by taking us through a process of consultation, collaboration, and deliberation. Sometimes she changed her mind and let us do it the way we preferred.

As the fourth grade progressed, on good days, when we were lucky and had been diligent and there was time before the dismissal bell would ring, we would gather ourselves up into our now familiar groups and speak our poems. With voices and bodies reverberating, we encountered a harmony that lifted us sometimes into the ridiculous (with Ogden Nash) and sometimes the sublime. We learned that the way you can get to that experience of being uplifted and held is through community, each one's voice supporting the other, each one's part a piece of the whole. Unlike singing choruses, in this chorus every voice was a good voice, and there was a part for every person. This chorus was bounded by the circle that drew you in and never needed to keep some out.

I heard about a recent survey of Americans asking them what they feared the most. More people were afraid of public speaking than of death. I also know that most Americans have difficulty experiencing themselves as good enough, adequate, and acceptable, craving always the approval or validation of an outside authority. And most Americans suffer in loneliness because they have believed the myths of individualistic self-reliance and tried to go it alone. I am not like most Americans. I am not afraid of public speaking, of teaching, reciting, moving into the rhythms of poetry, the realms of the ridiculous or the sublime. I have found the place inside myself that has the power to validate, admire, and approve of who I am and what I do. And wherever I am and whatever I do, I live and act in community. In that community context resides my strength, my wisdom, and my best self.

That is an awful lot to have taught a fourth-grader, even if I had never grasped long division. But I did that too. It was a year that transformed me, grew me deep as well as up. Mrs. Lewis, more than forty years have lapsed since then. But it is not too late to whisper, "Thank you."

P.S. This was more than forty years ago. Mrs. Lewis is probably not alive to read this. But if she is, I want her to know that the name I had when I sat in her class was Anita Klein.

ॐ Ossie Davis and Ruby Dee

From With Ossie and Ruby:
In This Life Together

At Center High, I could not wait to get my hands on my textbooks, which I read from top to bottom as soon as they fell into my hands. Wilhelmina Gaines was my English teacher. She spoke as if her words tasted sweet, and because of her, I learned the joys of listening to speech and language in a different way. She was tall, and brown, with long, black hair that fell to her shoulders. I think she wore glasses, and some of her teeth were gold. In her company, you felt ashamed not to be dressed as well as she was, not to be as clean, to smell as fresh, and not to sparkle as brightly in the eye as she did. We all loved Mrs. Gaines. We couldn't help ourselves.

ॐ John L. Johnson

My Lifeline

Each morning while shaving, I catch a glimpse of my eyes staring back at me. I ask a familiar question: "How did I get here?" I graduated with honors from an Ivy League college and received a master's and a doctorate from another highly selective institution. I have held several responsible jobs. But why am I not on drugs, in prison or dead?

My mother owned a whorehouse outside the main gates of a U.S. Army base in Korea. I never met my father. When I was five, a soldier (who I thought was my real father) brought me to the United States; my mother stayed behind.

This man, a high school dropout and petty criminal, and I lived like gypsies, moving from boardinghouse to boardinghouse once every one or two months, when we couldn't pay rent. We slept on subway trains that traveled from Brooklyn to the Bronx.

I know how I got there to here. I got here because of my teachers.

My first-grade teacher took care of me when my father was in jail. My third-grade teacher, Miss Celine, gave me odd jobs after school, and she talked often to me about family, hard work, and the importance of school.

In the seventh grade, Miss Mill helped me believe I had the potential to be a good student, perhaps go to college and make something of myself.

In the eighth grade, Mr. Hamlet talked each day after football practice about honor, dignity, courage, and victory—things I had never heard about in my neighborhood.

Everything I have and everything I am I owe to my teachers.

To all teachers who think about leaving the profession because they wonder what good they are doing: I hope you think about my life and story. Yes, you are underpaid, overworked and must deal with all the political issues surrounding your work as well as parents who are in many cases just children themselves.

Know that although it may not be immediately evident, you are getting through to your students, you are being heard, you are making a difference, and you and your efforts will never, ever be forgotten.

♂ Faye Wade Henning
To My Teachers, "Well Done!"

There is very little in my memory bank about teachers who taught me between the second and fifth grades, but there is a great deal about my sixth-grade teacher. By that grade, much to my dismay, I had been firmly established as a bright student. The reputation was an albatross because I did not want to be noticed for anything. I just wanted to go to school, do my work, be left alone, and go home. So when I was selected to represent my school in the annual spelling bee, I cried for days and begged my mother to tell the teacher that I could not participate. My tears did not work. I saw a way out of my dilemma when the principal let it be known that he wanted his niece to have this honor. In the trial spelling bee that was held to make the determination, I deliberately missed a word. I was ecstatic! The principal's niece, not me, would represent the school in the big event. I thought I had pulled off the intentional error, but my teacher knew. She knew what I had done.

She insisted that I accompany her to the official bee and that I sit next to her. She knew what was going to happen. Early in the bee, on the second round, our school's representative missed an easy word, *carburetor*. My teacher turned to me and said, "You would not have missed that word." That was all she said, and all she needed to say. I felt like a shamed Atlas who had deliberately let the world crash to the ground and shatter into pieces. By insisting that I attend the bee, my teacher taught me about responsibility and courage and integrity. What I did when I deliberately missed a word in the trial bee was dishonest. It was a betrayal of my parents' belief and trust in me. They had made education, success, and achievement priorities for my sister and me. It was a diminishing of myself and an act of ingratitude, for I had been blessed with abilities I chose not to use. My teacher was right. I would not have missed *carburetor*. Again, it was a teacher who taught me the importance of courage. It was a teacher who believed in me. It was a teacher who made me promise myself that I would never give less of who or what I was. Later, Mr. Thompson in the eighth grade and Mr. Nat D. Williams in high school would reaffirm this lesson.

Today, as an assistant principal in a large urban high school, I hope I am doing justice to all of my teachers, especially those who said *no* to my decision not to use my gifts or to be socially popular rather than academically serious. I hope they are pleased with the care I have taken of their legacy of hard work and achievement. I hope I am providing students with belief in themselves as my teachers did for me many years ago. I owe them so much, so very much. I hope they are pleased with my work. I hope they are saying, "Well done."

✤ Robin D. G. Kelley
First Crush

I fell in love for the first time in the fall of 1970. Well, actually, it was more like the third time if you count my mom and a girl named Starling whom I met in the first grade. But this was different. I was eight years old, far more mature than others my age, more worldly, well beyond afternoon naps and Crayola valentines. The object of my affections was about three times my age, nearly twice my height, cooler than any girl I knew, possessed movie star beauty and urban hipness, and knew everything about everything. I could barely hide my disappointment on the first day of class when she wrote her name on the board: *Mrs.* Jane Andrias.

First crushes are always immediate, always love at first sight. And I was not the only one to fall for our new third-grade teacher. Boys and girls alike—the good ones, the "bad" ones —were completely enamored with Mrs. Andrias (whom we called "Miss Andrias" less out of defiance than linguistic ease). None of us had had a young teacher before, let alone one who was enthusiastic and genuinely excited about education. Mrs. Klein, a tall, stiff, expressionless disciplinarian with a heavy German accent, had tolerated no crumbs during snack time and demanded absolute silence during nap time. Evidently, I failed to make a favorable impression on Mrs. Klein because she had me placed in a first-grade class for "slow learners" under the iron fist of a Miss Lavitan. She made Mrs. Klein look like Denise Nicholas on the hit TV show *Room 222*. Miss Lavitan ran the class like a maximum-security prison, employing an elaborate system of punishment and reward to maintain order. Learning was secondary, and unfortunately we never got beyond a primary mode of existence. I'm still haunted by the memory of Miss Lavitan forcing some kid to stand in the wastepaper basket and repeat the words "I'm garbage" until he learned his lesson. I don't recall what the lesson was, but he must have learned something to be released from the "hole." I looked forward to second grade because I had heard nice things about Mrs. Porter, an older, dignified African-American teacher who had a reputation for being stern yet encouraging. Just my luck: She fell seriously ill two weeks into the new term, leaving us to do battle with a yearlong parade of inadequate substitutes.

To fully comprehend the excitement we felt for Mrs. Andrias, one must know the broader context. P.S. 28 still sits on a slice of 155th Street, nestled between Amsterdam and St. Nicholas, a section of the Washington Heights neighborhood at the northern edge of Harlem. In 1970, before the massive migration of Dominicans, the vast majority of students were African-American or Puerto Rican, and nearly all of us were poor. In this community of latchkey kids, our parents (frequently mothers) labored long hours simply to afford the rotting produce from the corner grocers and to pay rent on substandard tenement apartments or dimly lit high-rise projects. We had to make a life in small places crowded with siblings and pests, rusty tap water, radiators that worked intermittently during the coldest of winters, and few windows to relieve us from the summer heat. Of course, we had fire escapes—poor people's terraces—and innumerable ways to escape the fire of ghetto life. We had block parties, fire hydrants blasting cool water on overheated ashy brown bodies, the corner candy store (which tragically doubled as a retail outlet for heroin) where loose change got us Pixy Stix, Good & Plenty's, caramel squares, jaw breakers, Red Ropes, and huge chunks of bubble gum. Who could forget the dulcet melody of the Mr. Softee truck turning onto 156th and Broadway, peddling mounds of Soft Serve ice cream covered with sprinkles?

Beyond the visceral pleasures of street life in Harlem and Washington Heights, we lived during an era when Blackness was a badge of pride. Besides the Spanish and English that had dominated our community for decades, phrases in Ki-swahili flowed comfortably from the lips of older, Afro-coifed brothers and sisters. "Habari Gani" was almost as common as "What's happenin'!" Dashikis were in effect, and for a brief moment many of us drank a beverage called Afro-Cola—the taste of freedom! More to the point, the politicization of the Black community also spread to the schools. When I entered third grade, P.S. 28 was already embroiled in an intense community struggle to reduce overcrowding. Classrooms designed for thirty-five students were accommodating as many as fifty, a problem exacerbated by the fact that resources for inner-city schools were already scarce.

There were bigger problems. Less than two years earlier, the public school system had blown up over race and community control. During the fall of 1968, the United Federation of Teachers (UFT) walked off their jobs after Mayor John Lindsay and the Board of Education granted community control to the residents of the Ocean Hill–Brownsville section of Brooklyn. The predominantly Black and Puerto Rican community there wanted a voice in personnel and curriculum issues, for they (with support from the African-American Teachers Association) regarded most white educators and their programs as paternalistic and out of touch with the needs of inner-city children. Challenging the prevailing view of poor Black and Puerto Rican kids as educationally disadvantaged or impaired, leaders of the community control movement believed that teachers of their own race were needed to help build self-esteem and create a healthier environment for effective learning. As a result, when the community board attempted to reassign nineteen white teachers, the UFT under Albert Shanker called for a strike, which ultimately killed the community control program. It also generated enormous tensions between Black teachers and communities and the progressive, mostly Jewish teachers who had been committed to teaching urban children of color. Many felt betrayed by the community control board, particularly since UFT-affiliated teachers were responsible for developing a pluralistic curriculum that incorporated African-American history.

As a kid, I didn't know any of this. I knew about overcrowding because my sister and I joined our mother on marches outside the school. I knew I was Black and proud and the pigs were not to be trusted and I was part of the Third World and white folks were the world's minority and that Dr. King and Malcolm and Gandhi (that's another story!) had died for us. But I had no idea that Mrs. Andrias, our angel, the love of my life, had just entered the lion's den. After all, she was young, progressive, and Jewish, and she loved teaching *us*. I don't believe she supported Shanker, nor do I think she was completely opposed to community control, but these issues had very little relevance to what she was attempting to do. Armed with teaching methods unfamiliar to both her colleagues and our parents, she shook things up in ways that were independent of these warring factions.

Her first act was to create an "open classroom." The room was divided into work spaces designated by areas of study— math, reading, social studies, science, arts, and so on. We could do whatever we wanted as long as we spent sufficient time on each topic. Although my memory of the details is vague, the sense of freedom we felt, the excitement of discovery was simply overwhelming. We did not sit at desks and listen to our teacher drone on all day about fractions or antonyms or the Bill of Rights. We worked in groups, solved problems, played math games, sculpted in clay, and wrote poetry. Lots of poetry. And we came together as a whole class to discuss one thing or another —contemporary politics, a school play, a book, poem, or painting, a fight in the playground. But we were rarely lectured to.

I never said much in these discussions, being extremely shy and soft-spoken. Years later, Mrs. Andrias reminded me of something I had said in class. Apparently, she had read a poem and asked us what it meant. All of the other kids offered literal interpretations of the text. She called on me and I went straight for the metaphoric: "It's about death," I whispered. I was right. She never forgot that. I could not overcome my shyness back then, but I made up for my lack of classroom participation by volunteering to help Mrs. Andrias after school. I lived three blocks away and walked home by myself, so staying after was no big deal. Initially, I offered to erase the board and clean the erasers. I then began to push chairs in, pick up things off the floor, take on any kind of job just to extend the day. She, in turn, would ask about my mother, tell me a story about her family, introduce me to a new book or poet or artist, ask me questions about class, or work alongside me in silence. I lived for those after-school moments and tried to stretch them as long as I could. More than once she had to gently tell me to go home, which nearly brought me to tears.

My volunteer job became my obsession. For a while I stayed after every day, until others in the class got hip to my little oasis. It felt like an invasion; soon five, six, seven kids were staying after to help. I couldn't find an eraser to clean or a chair to move or any little task that would justify my presence. And being shy and unassertive, I was elbowed out of the safety of Mrs. Andrias's classroom and back to our empty apartment, or in the care of my big sister and her friends, or in the living rooms of neighbors who watched us while my mom and grandmother worked.

In hindsight, I think our teacher needed space and our staying after was probably more of a hindrance than anything else, though she always treated our volunteerism with warmth and gratitude. I've since learned that Mrs. Andrias spent that year under tremendous pressure. Her colleagues viciously attacked her teaching methods, and several parents thought her approach was too radical. I can only imagine what went on in their heads: *These ghetto kids need fundamentals—reading, writing, arithmetic—not poetry and art. Freedom? These hardheaded niggas need discipline.* My mother was one of Mrs. Andrias's staunch defenders, but beyond providing moral support I don't think she was all that effective. As the resident flower child of 157th and Amsterdam, my mother simply had no political clout in the 'hood. A high school dropout and autodidact of the highest order, she read Simone de Beauvoir and the Bhagavad Gita, practiced meditation and yoga, wore her hair out and wild long before Chaka Kahn came on the scene, and she sometimes walked the streets of Harlem barefoot. I'm sure the enemy wrote my mom off as a crazy hippie before she could say a word in Mrs. Andrias's defense.

Besides hostility outside of the classroom, Mrs. Andrias had to manage children who were weighed down by enormous inner turmoil. Ironically, because she created a safe space for free expression, some kids chose her classroom to vent years of pent-up anger, frustration, and fear. She encouraged us to express ourselves with paint brushes and pencils, which we did. Except that some kids applied these tools upside each other's heads rather than to the rolls of butcher paper Mrs. Andrias provided. I remember one guy, in particular, who was always rolling on the floor duking it out with classmates and even swinging on our teacher. He was the smallest kid in the class, but the boy could do damage. He kicked, scratched, swung wildly, and made contact often. I cried the day he knocked Mrs. Andrias's glasses off of her nose and tore her stockings. I cried because she cried; for just a split second she seemed on the verge of giving up, of calling it quits. I had seen my mother's tears on many nights, but never had I seen a teacher cry. I thought teachers were invincible, or worse, that they were beyond feelings. But Mrs. Andrias cared deeply for the entire class, and all she wanted was for us to fall in love with knowledge, to discover the world around us and turn to our imaginations to create new worlds, to know that we were all intellectuals with the capacity to think.

By the time I finished third grade in June of 1971, I was completely and hopelessly in love, but the object of my romantic energies had shifted from my teacher to a lifelong passion for intellectual work—especially teaching and writing. Mrs. Andrias turned out to be more of a matchmaker than an eight-year-old's dream date, for she introduced me to the power of words and gave me the most valuable lessons I have ever received as a writer. She taught me that writing is not a chore but a work of art, a sculpture made of words. Like any sculpture, it needs a foundation, an architecture that will hold it together, but what you do with it depends on your imagination. Writing can startle, it can animate dreams, it can create spaces for freedom, it can caress and tease, and it can administer a beat down. She also taught us to appreciate honest criticism. We learned to correct ourselves, to edit, to begin again, and in the process we discovered new knowledge and beautiful possibilities in our mistakes.

Above all, Mrs. Andrias *made us take responsibility for our own education.* Her open classroom gave us freedom to pursue knowledge in our own way, but it placed an enormous responsibility on us to balance time and work we were expected to do. Although we studied in small groups, we worked independently and were encouraged to look beyond what was available to us in the classroom. We engaged and synthesized material, put ideas into practice through art, writing, experiments, model building, and a variety of other projects. Sometimes an exciting discovery kept me from leaving the science station; other times, a particularly frustrating equation tied me to the math station for what seemed like an eternity. By day's end, I had worked to nourish myself, and all that nourishment left me even hungrier.

Learning to take responsibility for our own knowledge lay at the heart of Mrs. Andrias's approach to teaching. Each of us was expected to become an active learner, a self-motivated and independent researcher, and an imaginative thinker. In other words, as a third-grader I discovered something many of my own university students today have not figured out: Knowledge is not passively given but actively pursued.

I lost contact with Mrs. Andrias after the summer of 1971. My father decided he wanted his children to live with him and his new wife in Seattle, so our summer visit turned into a forced exile that lasted over six years—much to my poor mother's anguish. We arrived just in time to participate in Seattle's school busing program, which put my sister and me in a hostile all-white suburban school about an hour outside of the city's Central District. My teachers at Loyal Heights Elementary School initially placed us in "da-poor-dumb-underprivileged-ghetto-Negro" category, despite the fact that my fourth-grade classmates were doing work we had done in the second grade. And the white kids didn't know whether to hate or fear me (although they did get a rude awakening on the playground when they fought over me for first pick in touch football; five minutes into the game, they had to question their assumptions about Black athletic prowess).

I survived public education, even had at least one other wonderful teacher in high school after moving to California, but my memories of Mrs. Andrias always loomed large. After the publication of my first book in 1990, I looked her up simply to thank her for her role in making me who I am. She was easy to find; every progressive person involved in New York public education knew or at least had heard of Jane Andrias of Central Park East I (CPE I). The school was renowned and so was Mrs. Andrias. When we met at CPE I, she was teaching art, surrounded by a bevy of bright-eyed and talkative students who floated in and out of the room in a state of utter joy. In addition, she had just been appointed acting principal—a post she continues to hold as of this writing (although she's no longer "acting"). And she was writing—producing papers and talks and articles rethinking educational practice, doing intellectual work that doesn't simply interpret the world but tries to change it.

Put simply, Mrs. Andrias amazed me with all of her energy,

her accomplishments, her vision. Despite my Ph.D., my newly published book, and my university professorship, I felt like a little boy again. Although two decades had passed, she knew exactly who I was and recalled many details about my participation in her class. She also brought me up to speed about what happened at P.S. 28 after I left. Her tenure there had not lasted much longer. A group (more like a posse) of teachers, administrators, and parents had mobilized against her in what must have felt like a bona fide witch hunt. She eventually landed on her feet but only after a difficult row.

Thank goodness she stayed the course, for I can only imagine how many lives she must have changed, how many brilliant minds she must have nurtured, how many children she must have cured of intellectual narcolepsy, how much turmoil she must have tamed, and how many of these kids, like me, are still in love.

 ⁂ Mary C. Lewis

Awakening

To a child, twelve years represents a lifetime, more than long enough to develop a thick-skinned numbness, as I had. By 1966 I'd erected the equivalent of a fortress around myself. Now and then, awareness flickered and flared like candlelight in a drafty castle, but mostly I shielded myself within a sleepwalker's existence. Twelve years of misguided parenting had caused me to pull up the gate, drain the moat, and ban all visitors. When I look back on my childhood, I visualize the confinement I'd constructed, and I see with an adult's perception how fragile the enclosure was. And I marvel at the phenomenon of my seventh-grade teacher's entrance.

She was stunning. She stood in the classroom doorway on my first day of seventh grade, newly arrived at my school. The pinnacle of her French-rolled hairstyle grazed the top of the door; some six feet below, the spikes of her high-heeled shoes straddled the doorsill. At her midpoint were arms right-angled to her shoulders and waist. In another outfit, gender, and era she could have depicted a gunslinger. She had an Amazon's skin and height, emanating attributes I'd read about in a library book: majestic, defender of the weak. *Have you come,* a voice inside me whimpered, *to rescue me?* My shell, the gatekeeper, shoved the query back to its dungeon and donned a mask of custom. Behind the mask, my eyes became introverted. Observation camouflaged misery.

There was much to absorb about the new teacher. Her hairstyle spurred a mental voyage to Brigitte Bardot. I remembered spying a magazine feature on Bardot at a neighborhood drugstore. Contrasts emerged. The teacher's hair color resembled the terra-cotta bungalows in my neighborhood. Although her knit dress displayed Bardot's cola bottle curves, the teacher had a stance that looked as hard to break as a brick. Magazine photos of the teacher lounging in a cleavage-revealing swimsuit seemed unlikely. My mental catalog of her refused to collate. Somehow a knight had mated with an Amazon and the result mixed Billy the Kid with an adult's-only film star. What sort of teacher was she?

"My name is Mrs. Honoré." She closed the door and stepped to the front of the room. "I used to teach at a school in Cabrini-Green." A buzz swatted back and forth, cupped behind awed hands.

"That's a project, right?"

"Yeah, on the North Side."

Cabrini-Green: a housing project far removed from my neighborhood. I lived in Chatham, on Chicago's South Side, amid prim lawns and modest houses. My mother, paraphrasing the sociologist E. Franklin Frazier, called our community "the mink-coated ghetto." Although we had the money to live wherever we chose, she explained we did not have all the options we should have possessed. Powerful people used our Blackness to block many of our choices. We lived in a ghetto, as did Blacks in Cabrini-Green. But Chatham was not a slum. I knew enough at twelve to know the difference between the two communities. Family members, neighbors, and news reports supplied the details. Cabrini-Green housed people with wallets too thin to afford houses. Families lived stacked on top of each other, in concrete towers with pavement for lawns. Someone, I didn't know who, thought it was acceptable for people to live like that. From within my personal fortress, where emotions eked out a withered existence, I felt bad for Cabrini-Green's residents—especially the children. To live there must have pinched.

A boy muttered, "Only the baddest of the bad live in the projects." A wolf-at-the-door quiver shot through me. If my classmate was correct, survival in Cabrini-Green featured a battle with poverty *and* danger. Only a warrior could have spent time there and lived to tell the tale. No wonder the new teacher displayed a gunfighter's spunk.

"Got a cousin there," mumbled another boy, Ronald. "Made me wish I had Mr. Smith and Mr. Wesson along when I went to visit." He squeezed his upper arm; burgeoning muscle swelled the sleeve of his shirt.

"I bet you did okay," said a classmate, Derrick. The hair-trigger glances he and Ronald flicked at Mrs. Honoré seemed to speculate on going toe to toe with her.

"I will kick your butt if you mess with me."

The buzz ended in mid-rustle. Showdown time. Inside the vault in my mind, reels of imagery became tangled. Amazons from South America jostled with gun-toters from the Wild West and other fighters, the Mau Mau of Kenya I had also read about. But most of those warriors were men. My new teacher asserted definitive womanliness. Notions of gender were reconfiguring. According to my mother, women should display the mantle of propriety. They should use the gentlest vocabulary and leave the brawling to men. I pictured Mrs. Honoré slamming Ronald and Derrick against a wall, hoisting them to eye level, her hand around each boy's throat. And yet her name and her body resounded with exotica.

Genteel or not, she faced a motley group: twelve-, thirteen-, and fourteen-year-olds known by the rest of the school as the "dummy" class. Derrick and Ronald were not the only undesirables. Ever since kindergarten, low grades on report cards and low scores on achievement tests kept the group ineligible for the "smart" class. A double whammy had landed me among the "dummies": my twin brother Berry scored higher than I did and the school system forbade placing twins in the same classroom. My classmates were a hodgepodge. Some kids, like myself, maintained decent grades but scored poorly on tests. Other kids excelled at one or two skills—art for a few, music for others—and wobbled enough at the so-called basics to stymie scholastic progress. The ebb and flow of our desire to learn forced us to weather a tradition of grouping kids according to a system of scores and rankings. Individual strengths and weaknesses had little to do with who were my classmates.

Our collective history included a September morning in fifth grade when the teacher asked about summer vacation. Derrick shocked her into silence with his description of juvenile detention, at the Audy Home. The same year, I hit Ronald upside the head with an unabridged dictionary after he teased me about wearing eyeglasses. New to the neighborhood, he didn't know I'd spent three miserable years begging my parents to purchase those glasses for me. He didn't know I had the nerve to pummel him with a five-pound book; neither did I. After that scrape he and I had a truce, as did the entire class by the end of sixth grade. We coexisted in a gutter of expectations: gang membership for some, teenage parenthood for others, unremarkable employment for most.

Seventh grade was a holding pen from which we would drift to eight grade. The school principal had a throw-up-her-hands approach to us. Maybe we'd get through high school and maybe we wouldn't. Evidently, the safety net of a Chatham address contained rips with our names on them, and someday—despite our battered shields of swaggers and slouches—fate would finish us off. We'd tumble out of the sac of Chatham and submerge in a world willing to keep us dumb and down. Some of us reacted to failure to meet academic standards by lashing out with misdeeds. Others tossed and turned through schooldays awash in boredom. Both reactions widened the holes in the safety net, making the likelihood of falling through a fait accompli.

Into this maelstrom strode Mrs. Honoré, with her war record at Cabrini-Green.

She circled the room. Whispers and snickers returned and rose to a din that blunted the *thwack* of her high-heeled shoes against the floorboards. Mayhem threatened. Habit was luring the group onto the battlefield of us versus them, the irredeemable versus the overseers. I kept quiet, out of curiosity more than politeness. Other teachers' steering had slipped from bad to worse. The fourth-grade teacher shoved misbehaving students under her desk. The fifth-grade teacher struck sass-talking kids with a yardstick. What would be this teacher's weapon?

"At the end of every school day," she said, "we're going to talk about sex."

Silence erupted, spilling over the room and heaving the group of kids backward in a single display of shock. Bardot's celluloid picture looped around my thoughts. A tingling began to sting me, pricking me out of my numbness. We're going to talk about *sex*?

Mrs. Honoré listed the schedule on the blackboard: English,

social studies, art, mathematics, other subjects. This year and the next, she explained, we would experience an interdepartmental program, a high school type of movement from room to room. A mole just below her cheekbone lifted and dimples appeared. "For the last half hour, you'll return here, to your homeroom. That's when we'll talk about sex. You can ask me anything you want."

She uttered that word again. *Sex* popped out and sat amid the schedule as though the school day had a place reserved for the topic. A ring of keys seemed to jangle outside the door to my innermost self. With her friendly dimples and her talk of interdepartmental scheduling and her offer to ask her anything—about *sex*—Mrs. Honoré had accessed an entranceway. My mother hadn't done that. She taught seventh- and eighth-graders at another school on the South Side. She hadn't talked to me about sex and hadn't mentioned putting sex into her lesson plans. Who did Mrs. Honoré think she was, sauntering in from a school in the slums and announcing regular instruction on, of all things, sex? She was threatening my stupor and, deep in a self-made dungeon, I cringed at the prospect of exposure.

In the last row sat the worst and the oldest classmates. They had the lowest grades and the most trips to the principal's office. Their reputation had inflated them to teenaged hoodlums. Fourteen-year-old Ronald sat among them and was their leader. He sprawled in a chair that was two sizes too small for him and blurted a question: "Can we talk about hemorrhoids?"

Students sniggered, seventh-grade minds ignorant of the question's pertinence. I joined in the laughter, breaking away from my internal struggle. Ronald swept the air with his hand as if to encourage kids' response. The back-talking clown in him had popped out before. Every September, teachers flinched when he lumbered into a classroom. It seemed he wore a placard on which "bad boy" was scrawled with a permanent marker. Usually the stuff tumbling from his mouth was silly, but he possessed the makings of a comedian. With Ronald around, life in the "dummy" class was lifted out of inertia.

Mrs. Honoré didn't seem to appreciate his humor. She moved toward him as if stalking her prey: *You dare to mess with an Amazon—Mau Mau who's conquered Cabrini-Green? I will win this fight,* her prowling promised, *not you.* She stood over him, silent, until the room quieted. The showdown climaxed. Ronald's overgrown hands shifted from forearms to chin. His face broadcast chagrin and resentment, as if his question entangled the "bad boy" placard around his neck. He couldn't make things right with Mrs. Honoré without ruining his reputation.

Her serenity contrasted with his fidgeting. Sure, she said, turning from him and facing the class, we could talk about hemorrhoids. She added other topics: male and female anatomy, how a female could and couldn't get pregnant. No question was stupid, she promised, and no topic was forbidden. Everyone listened, including Ronald. She'd tackled the showdown and hadn't thrown him against the wall or grounded him with ridicule. The battlefield of us against them faded into the past. The fight I was having with myself, involving the gatekeeper and the real me, subsided to a worrisome throb. Mrs. Honoré had arrived in my life and the lives of my classmates. Although she had yet to locate the key that would unlock my door, she hadn't given up on her search. She looked comfortable with her presence. I'd have to find a similar comfort level with her proximity.

&

Gradually, over time my classmates' questions became genuine rather than smart-alecky. I remained closemouthed, mask in place, continuing my observer's role. No, Mrs. Honoré declared in response to a girl's query, it wasn't true that "private parts" should be avoided. They needed daily washing and an interest in them was healthy, not harmful. Yes, she agreed on another afternoon, outbreaks of acne usually came during the teenage years. But resist the temptation to squeeze your pimples, she warned, or you'll have scars. Wash your face with a gentle cleanser, she advised, and suggested a couple of products. I noticed Ronald, one arm stretched across his desk, scribbling a note. A request, perhaps, for his mother's next trip to the grocery? He caught me watching him and his hand flew up to his chin. His buddies were teasing him lately about the bumps sprouting along his jaw. I shot him a grin to let him know I wouldn't tell anyone about his note taking. *It's all right,* I hoped my grin told him, *even a "bad boy" can listen and learn.*

The group's attitude was relaxing, but the change didn't occur overnight. One of Mrs. Honoré's first talks about sex, on the female reproductive system, did not go over well. As she calmly christened a diagram, using a yardstick to pinpoint each body part, girls squiggled in their seats. The diagram looked like a ram's head, dyed pink and shorn of wool. "Ooh, no" and "Uh-unh, that is ugly" echoed my own distaste. The ram's head didn't match my own insides, did it? *Vagina, uterus, Fallopian tubes* sounded like the cast and props of a science fiction movie. A wormy sensation slithered over me, reminiscent of when I watched *The Blob* and other creature feature films. I fought an urgent need to race to the bathroom and vomit. The battle over privacy, over disentombing me from my dungeon, renewed itself. At the time I could not have described the struggle that engaged me. Nor could I have named the opponents. At best I sensed alien forces at work, pod people with a ram's head and Mrs. Honoré's body, slinking into crevices I thought I'd sealed. It took every defense I possessed, of dispassion and lethargy, to remain seated, swallow my nausea, and let the gatekeeper rule.

And when Mrs. Honoré—still bland of face and moderate of tone—spoke about menstruation, a stink bomb may as well have exploded. Classmates crinkled their noses. According to the older girls, menstruation was rough: "Cramps is a doggone blankety-blank . . . a period is a dirty deal."

I couldn't take their comments to heart. I hadn't started having a "period" yet. My sister Vivian, three years older than I, never spoke about hers except to complain, mysteriously, about needing new panties. My mother never mentioned menstruation, either. Sometimes she fussed about not having something called "sanitary napkins" in the house and wouldn't say what they were. On those occasions, she sent me to a mom-and-pop store: "Tell Mrs. Vremis you need to buy Kotex for me. Not *Mr.* Vremis, *Mrs.* Vremis." Within the fretfulness with which she shooed me off to the store was a hands-off attitude toward sanitary napkins and their cause—menstruation. I felt more comfortable replenishing her stock of cigarettes.

The year before, when my brother David was born, I had wondered how babies were made. During my mother's pregnancy, her obvious physical change offered an opportunity to discuss reproduction with me. But she kept the opportunity out of bounds and instead focused on crankiness about how she and my father would afford a fifth child. My father, already employed as a fireman, took a second job at a nuts and bolts factory. Jokes about his extra labor—with the emphasis on *nuts*

—sputtered from Vivian and my older brother Greg. I didn't get the word play but my father did, whenever he overheard them. Their titters failed to amuse him. His temper ignited, throwing the household into conflagration. I retreated, as usual, reading tales set in faraway lands and squashing questions set in the here and now. It would take many years to understand that my confinement mimicked my mother's. Both of us coped with my father's temperament by imprisoning ourselves in isolation.

David's arrival revitalized my curiosity. One day, while my mother changed his diaper, I asked, "How do you know it's a boy?" She poked her finger at an anatomical part I didn't recognize, a thumb shape drooping between my newborn brother's legs. End of explanation and, apparently, sufficient for my aptitude. Instead, my chance viewing of a penis increased my stockpile of questions. *What was that thumblike thing called? Why did boys have one and girls didn't?* And so on. I lived in an era and in a family that shelved questions, on the cusp of sexual Puritanism and sexual liberation. Cram queries inside, my mother's example showed me: Don't ask and don't tell.

Like a toddler learning to talk, my inquisitiveness about sexuality grappled for a voice, hearing complaints and frankness and wondering which sounds made sense. My teacher offered every weekday afternoon some facts to strengthen my grasp of the world known as my body. *Learn.* I almost felt my brain cells stretching to take in new information. Mrs. Honoré's explanation sounded simple. Menstruation happened when an unfertilized egg left the female body through the vagina, along with blood and other substances built up in the uterus to nourish an embryo. About every twenty-eight days, if sperm didn't fertilize an egg, the menstrual cycle repeated itself. Why resist and curse?

Womanhood, to hear my teacher speak, was a-okay once a girl got the hang of body parts and twenty-eight-day cycles. But a lot of others disagreed, my sister and mother included. Whose opinion mattered most? Whose example should I follow? My thoughts flailed. Part of me recoiled, dismembered from classmates' embarrassment, uncertain about a teacher's offer, and distressed by a family's dysfunction. Change was afoot; I wasn't sure I could handle the alteration. The gatekeeper ridiculed my ability to leave my dungeon and flourish, insisting I belonged in the "dummy" class. In a voice endowed with shame, the gatekeeper posed questions that stalled me: What about the sneaky feeling that I knew more about sex than I let on? What about the stain infixed in me so deeply that I hid from its existence? What good were the facts Mrs. Honoré presented if they didn't cleanse?

&

Late one autumn night in eighth grade, I awoke with a damp nightgown. Had I, at age thirteen, wet the bed? With fingers that trembled, I probed the liquid. Even in the dark, I recognized the gook. Intermittent recklessness, when I'd scaled trees and jumped off jungle gyms, had familiarized me with blood. But this was different; this blood yanked me from sleep. This blood spurted from *down there,* in the unsanctioned terrain of *sex.* My brain scattered; logic hid. For several icy moments an avalanche of terror buried what Mrs. Honoré taught me. I thought I was dying. I tumbled out of bed, clutching the back of my nightgown and wondering if I left a trail of spatters that would tell of my last night on earth.

I tugged my mother down the stairs and asked, "Should we call a doctor?" A hospital seemed the place to take me. My knees shook. A chill mingled with a fever. Blood trickled along my legs as though life was leaving me. Why, I wanted to know, gripping my gown and staring at my mother, why didn't she do something about my plight? My mother *tsk-tsked* and took me by the elbow to the bathroom. She reached into the vanity cabinet under the sink and handed me an oblong, padded cloth with a gauze strip at each end. I held the cloth, speechless, uncertain what to do with it. I'd never seen a sanitary napkin before, never looked inside the box my mother stowed in the cabinet's farthest corner. I'd absorbed the information Mrs. Honoré passed along to me, but I hadn't absorbed her forthrightness. Instead, I'd floated into eight grade as though menstruation held no relevance for me. Despite my teacher's candidness, sanitary napkins existed where my mother stashed them: out of sight and unexplored.

I looked in the cabinet and recognized the sky blue box from my trips to the store. From then on I would be reaching into the box every month. My period had begun. My mother pulled an elastic strap from the cabinet drawer. "Put it on. And wash your nightgown." I thought I saw disgust on her face as she left the bathroom. The elastic contraption dangled from one hand, the sanitary napkin from the other. A few months before, I'd started wearing hosiery held up by a garter belt that resembled the strap. For several minutes I fumbled with the how-to of donning a sanitary napkin. Knots of pain sparred with my lower gut as I hunched over the sink, rinsing red from my gown. Tears joined the water. I felt like an infant forced to change her own diaper.

In spite of contractions that knifed through my belly, I went to school and sought out Mrs. Honoré. I needed her sympathy and remembered her expertise. But I was unsophisticated, unaware that approaching her signified the start of a change in me. I whispered my news, parroting what I'd heard the year before: Menstruation had dealt me a dirty deal. She soothed me with a hug and aspirin. "If the aspirin doesn't work, get some Midol. Menstruation is not a dirty deal. You'll be fine."

I wasn't sure about that. But even in my still drowsy condition, I suspected certainty wasn't the issue. I had moved on, to eighth grade and menstruation and growth. Mrs. Honoré's shared knowledge would have to serve as a staircase of remembrance. It was up to me to use the stairway and ascend from a subterranean quarantine. The climb was painful. Every month I suffered horrific cramps. A rash persisted along the bottom of my stomach that took years to abate. Without an allowance with which to purchase Midol, without a confidence that I was entitled to a remedy, my cure-all for cramps was to knead my belly with my fists. I dreaded the coming of each month's twenty-eighth day. Despite Mrs. Honoré's nearness down the hall at school, making progress felt like slogging through mire. It was difficult to pull myself away from one belief (that menstruation condemned me) and urge myself toward another belief (that menstruation affirmed me). Like any girl would, I wanted to lean on my mother for support. I asked her how she handled menstrual cramps. She shrugged and said childbirth ended them.

"But what did you do before? Didn't you have cramps when you were my age?"

"I don't remember."

"I've heard aspirin works." I decided not to mention Mrs. Honoré's help.

"Aspirin upsets the stomach. A few hours of discomfort won't hurt you."

&

It took me a long time to get over my mother's flubbing of my initiation into womanhood. And though the healing included laborious progress, overwhelming anger, and many flubs of my own, I did heal. In time, comfort replaced numbness regarding my sense of self. When I was twelve, a teacher introduced me to the beauty of self-acceptance. From then on, I began to see myself more clearly, and I awakened to a fuller view of my mother than the glimpses I held of her while I was stuck in my dungeon. I realized that her construct tolerated a trespasser like my father and a belief such as submission because to her, it seemed no other shelter was possible. If my mother had experienced the entrée of a teacher like Mrs. Honoré, perhaps she would have wed a safer man than my father and seen to it that her life with him featured parity rather than imbalance. I wouldn't have needed an oblivious, submerged existence; neither would she. Had she known what I learned from Mrs. Honoré, perhaps my mother would have discovered what life could offer outside an enclosure that ultimately chokes the life one seeks to protect. Nowadays, I hope I move with the enlightened outlook that began the year I met Yvonne Honoré.

⁋ Toby Perlman

From Teaching Genius: Dorothy DeLay
and the Making of a Musician

Who was the force? Who was the person we have to thank? Who was responsible? Miss DeLay took this boy [Itzhak Perlman], and she gave the world a gift. She presented him as a whole human being. By the time she was finished, he was a whole human being. How did she do it? Well, she did it as a teacher—scales and so on—but she also did it, most important, as a human being. She nurtured his interests, encouraged his interest in art, got his parents to get him an art tutor so that he could paint and draw. Took him to museums herself, took him to concerts herself, encouraged his interest in baseball—all the things that normal children are encouraged to do, all that came from her.

She knew that eventually his art would be a reflection of his life. Therefore, he'd better have a life! It all sounds easy —of course she did this and of course she did that—but it's not so, because other teachers do not do that. She saw the whole boy, the whole child, the whole situation, and she supported it. Everybody needs support, everybody needs a helping hand. She wasn't just in there for the lesson time. One of the things that she did—the most remarkable thing—was that she recognized that his disability was going to be a real problem in the eyes of the public. *She* knew that it was no problem at all—it was just no problem—but she saw the way people responded, and she understood that half the battle was going to be convincing the powers that be that this was a boy who could do anything, and she set about doing that.

She set up situations where my husband would appear alone, where people would see him by himself. The thing is that she knew—by that time I was in the picture—that of course he could be alone, what was the big deal? But there were people in our business who were very powerful, whose support he needed and he was not going to get. When I came into his life he was seventeen, almost eighteen, and in a way, I was the answer to her prayers. I don't know whether she approved of me as a mate for him—I think she did—but I was the answer, because here was this boy, this disabled boy who was just turning eighteen, who had a girl, and that was just the perfect kind of thing—for him to have a girlfriend.

She would see to it that he would go to concerts where she knew some of these people would be, and she made him go by himself, or he would go with me. It was not actually that she set up anything different than what he would have ordinarily done, but she made sure it happened in situations where people in the business—where Mr. Hurok, let's say—would look for Isaac [as Toby Perlman calls her husband] and his mother, and would see only Isaac, or Isaac and me. Miss DeLay made sure that that happened, so that by the time he went to the competition [the Leventritt competition, which launched Perlman's career in 1964 when he won it], it was kind of common knowledge that this was a pretty independent kid.

I feel very clear that she was the motivating force in his life, that she was the most important person in his life, and that she still is. I don't know how much in touch with Isaac she is, but I do know that the few times she has been ill nothing else exists for him—he is just on total alert. I don't know if he sees that in himself. When he sees her, all he does is yell at her. He picks on her mercilessly. It is like a child with a parent, a child who never came to grips with the parent as being imperfect. He is scowling all the time at her. "Why are you doing that and why are you doing this and why did you order that? That's a bad pasta, that's the wrong pasta. Don't get that, get this."

You know, this is a very complicated relationship. Isaac is so intensely involved with her in a way that I am sure he never looked at. He doesn't examine things that way, men don't do that. If I said to him, "I think you are terribly concerned with Miss DeLay, I think you need to think about it," he would say, "Don't be silly, I'm not at all worried about Miss DeLay. I just saw her the other day. She is fine. She is just fine." It is very childish in a way, defensive and the way a child is with a parent. And it is touching, it is very touching.

You see, I am not talking about how much she knows as a violin teacher. Although, let me tell you, this woman knows *soooo much*. She comes to a concert of my husband's and I get a list at the end of what is wrong. Not just what is wrong, because that's silly, I know what is wrong. She says, "You know, sugarplum, the violin is a little low—I don't like the position, I think he should move it over a little bit."

If I wait for the right moment and say, "You know, Miss DeLay mentioned to me—," he'll always say to me, "Did she like it? Did she like it? Did she like it? Was she happy? Did she think it was good?" Or, "What do you mean, she didn't come? What do you mean, she wasn't there?" The questions are of paramount importance. I might say, a week or so later, "You know, Miss DeLay mentioned something to me about your position."

"She did? What did she say?" He is very open. If she said it directly, he'd probably be very defended. "Well, she doesn't know anything. Blaaah"—you know. That is why she tells it to me.

The other thing about Miss DeLay is she has the most incredible mind. Her mind is the mind of youth. Searching all the time. Never thinking she knows everything. Wondering and questioning and listening. She is so interested in everything. I think it comes from being with young people. It keeps her so young. When I talk to her, I feel she's younger than I am. I think it comes from this joyful aspect of her.

This exuberance, her quest for knowledge, all of that, she has it within herself, in her daily life, in the way she approaches her teaching—but she made that essential to him. She gave it to him as a gift. Be inquisitive, enjoy everything, learn everything, do everything. She gave him a kind of taste for life and a zest for things. I don't want to say that—that's not fair—it's not fair to say she gave that to him. I think he had that, but she encouraged it.

He won the Leventritt and he began to play, and right away he got management. Overnight he was embraced by everyone in the music world. Now, it was a world that musically we were both ready for. I had no problem musically, but in every other way, there were so many issues. In the early years of my marriage, I saw Miss DeLay all the time. She was a constant source, a constant resource, because I needed advice all the time. I was always on the phone or in her studio getting instructions about how to deal with this unfamiliar life. I could not have done it without her. Little things—"Do I write a thank-you note to so-and-so?" "No, sugar, you write a thank-you note to this one but not to that one." Isaac would be away and I would have dinner with Miss DeLay, I would have lunch with her. This was totally away from the violin, this was as a friend, as an adviser, and still as the lady who was in charge.

✎ Langston Hughes

From The Big Sea: An Autobiography

I went to Central High School in Cleveland. We had a magazine called the *Belfry Owl*. I wrote poems for the *Belfry Owl*. We had some wise and very good teachers, Miss Roberts and Miss Weimer in English, Miss Chesnutt, who was the daughter of the famous colored writer, Charles W. Chesnutt, and Mr. Hitchcock, who taught geometry with humor, and Mr. Ozanne, who spread the whole world before us in his history classes. Also Clara Dieke, who painted beautiful pictures and who taught us a great deal about many things that are useful to know—about law and order in art and life, and about sticking to a thing until it is done.

Ethel Weimer discovered Carl Sandburg for me. Although I had read of Carl Sandburg before—in an article, I think, in the *Kansas City Star* about how bad free verse was—I didn't really know him until Miss Weimer in second-year English brought him, as well as Amy Lowell, Vachel Lindsay, and Edgar Lee Masters, to us. Then I began to try to write like Carl Sandburg.

✇ Nikki Giovanni

Miss Delaney Was Right

I actually think it is my basic nervousness that has always made my handwriting so poor. Well, my handwriting is not poor but it is clearly not the beautiful work of art that others have. My grandfather had a beautiful hand. His letters were perfectly formed with just a touch of flourish to show individuality but not so much that vanity crept in. My grandmother had a serious hand, her letters bold, clear, one might even say strident. You knew it was from Grandmother from quite a distance away. Mommy also has a very nice hand with a bit more flourish than Grandpapa, her father. Mommy always likes to break words up with curlicues, which I have always admired. But me, well, I never was even good with a pen. There has never been a happier person than when ball point pens became affordable and people like me did not have to suffer through pen and ink.

One of my favorite teachers, if not my very favorite, Miss Alfredda Delaney, always encouraged me in my writing but she would also say, "You must take typing. You will never be a writer unless you learn to type." At first I was hurt because I couldn't see what typing had to do with creating but I learned. Miss Brice taught typing, and the problem with all the skill-based subjects is that there is no room for mistakes. I would be extremely discouraged because I was not nearly as fast as a lot of my fellow and sister students. I am still not quick but Miss Delaney would say "You must stick with it" and because I really did adore Miss Delaney, I kept trying.

Mommy gave me an electric typewriter the year I went off

to college. Miss Delaney was very proud and extolled again the importance of typing. I started typing my papers in college, more because Miss Delaney had convinced me my handwriting was unacceptable than because I believed in the power of typing. I also began rather seriously to write and, by cracky, Miss Delaney was right! My grades were better. I knew better what I was saying. My papers looked better. And I became a writer. About twenty years later Miss Delaney introduced me at a writers' conference with this story. And I am so happy that she was so very right.

❧ ❧ ❧ THREE

Leading by Example

We learn by doing and we learn best by teaching.
❧ Derrick Bell,
law professor, author, and activist

From a Conversation
with Howard Zinn

I think teachers should be honest with students. Say to them, "Look, this is where I stand," while at the same time making it clear to them that this is not where you have to stand. There are different viewpoints, different ways of looking at the world, but I want you to know my way, and I want you to understand why I feel this way. I don't want you to be afraid to say "I disagree with you" or "This is my point of view." Only then will our conversations be interesting. It's actually a delicate balance, because on the one hand you want to be honest and state your viewpoint. On the other hand, you don't want to intimidate the students into accepting it.

Sometimes the way I do it is just to say, "Look, I'm going to tell you very bluntly how I feel about things. I don't feel ashamed to do this, because I feel that you're not a blank slate. I'm not the first influence on you. You came into my classroom loaded and bombarded with information from previous teachers, from television, newspapers, your parents, and from the world outside, so I'm not worried that I am taking a blank slate and imprinting my message on it. But I assume that what I am going to tell you is not what you have heard before. I'm going to tell you something different because I assume you have not been brought up in the free marketplace of ideas. Of course, the marketplace of ideas has been dominated by certain ideas in the culture. And these ideas you've heard again and again, like you must serve your country in war. That's a dominant idea in our culture."

A teacher teaches as much, if not more, by what he or she does in the world than by what he or she says in the classroom. I remember when I was teaching in 1960 and 1961, when the sit-ins were starting. I felt that I could talk to my students about civil rights, racial equality, the Constitution, the Fourteenth Amendment, the Fifteenth Amendment, the idea of democracy, the idea of equality. I could talk about this endlessly in my classroom, but what if my students went out into the city of Atlanta and they started to put those ideas into practice? What if they picketed, demonstrated, sat-in, and got arrested? What if they acted on those ideals only to see that their teacher was still behind in the classroom preparing for the next day's lesson? Well, I think that would weaken, considerably weaken, the teaching. I think that my students at Spelman College learned more from the fact that I was often there with them. They knew that I supported them, that I was sitting-in too, that I was demonstrating too. That said to them, "It's not enough to talk about the wonderful principles. You really have to act on them."

&❧ Marian Wright Edelman

From Lanterns: A Memoir of Mentors

Howard Zinn and I arrived at Spelman College together in 1956. He and his wife Roslyn and their two children, Myla and Jeff, lived in the back of the Spelman College infirmary where students felt welcome to gather, explore ideas, share hopes, and just chew the fat.

Howie encouraged students to think outside the box and to question rather than accept conventional wisdom. He was a risk-taker. I am indebted to him for my first interracial experience with a discussion group at the YMCA on international relations and for going with his Black Spelman students to sit in the "White" section of the state legislature which stopped its deliberations to hoot and jeer and demand that we be removed. He lost no opportunity to challenge segregation in theaters, libraries, and restaurants, and encouraged us to do the same.

Howie not only lived what he taught in history class by breaching Atlanta's segregated boundaries, but stretched my religious tolerance beyond childhood limits. I felt shock and confusion when he announced in class that he did not believe in Jesus Christ. There were few Jewish citizens in my small South Carolina hometown. Through him I began to discern that goodness comes in many faiths and forms which must be respected and honored.

The Black Spelman establishment did not like Howard Zinn any more than the White establishment did. Later, after he joined the faculty at Boston University, its president, John Silber, disliked him just as much as Spelman's president Albert Manley did, because he made some teachers and administrators uncomfortable by challenging the comfortable status quo. We called him Howie and felt him to be a confidant and friend as well as a teacher, contrary to the more formal and hierarchical traditions of many Black colleges. He stressed analysis, not memorization; questioning, discussions, and essays rather than multiple choice tests and pat answers; and he conveyed and affirmed my Daddy's belief and message that I could do and be anything and that life was about far more than bagging a Morehouse man for a husband.

He lived simply and nonmaterialistically. I felt comfortable asking to drive his old Chevrolet to transport picketers to Rich's department store. He was passionate about justice and his belief in the ability of individuals to make a difference in the world. Not a word-mincer, he said what he believed and encouraged us as students to do the same.

He conveyed to me and to other students that he believed in us. He conveyed to members of the Student Nonviolent Coordinating Committee whose voter registration and organizing efforts he chronicled in his book *SNCC: The New Abolitionists* that he believed in, respected, and supported our struggle. He was there when two hundred students conducted sit-ins and seventy-seven of us got arrested. He provided us a safe space in his home to plan civil rights activities by listening and not dictating. He laughed and enjoyed life just as he still does and he spoke up for the weak and little people against the big and powerful people just as he still does.

An eloquent chronicler of *The People's History of the United States,* of the Civil Rights Movement, and of the longings of the young and the poor and the weak to be free, his most profound message and the title of one of his books is that "you can't be neutral on a moving train." You can and must act against injustice.

Howie taught me to question and ponder what I read and heard and to examine and apply the lessons of history in the context of daily political, social, and moral challenges like racial discrimination and income inequality. He combined book learning with experiential opportunities to engage in interracial discussions; partnered with community groups challenging legal segregation; and engaged students as participants, observers, data collectors, and witnesses in pending legal cases. He listened and answered questions as we debated strategies for conducting sit-in demonstrations to challenge segregated public dining facilities and used his car to check out, diagram, and help choreograph planned civil rights events. He reassured us of the rightness of our cause when uncertainty and fear crept in and some of our college presidents sought to dampen our spirits and discourage our activities.

In short, he was there for us through thick and thin, focused not just on our learning in the classroom but on our learning to stand up and feel empowered to act and change our own lives and the community and region in which we lived. He taught us to be neither victims nor passive observers of unjust treatment but active and proud claimants of our American birthright.

ℊ Mary Alice Hubbard McWilliams

Yes, They Could!
And Yes, They Did!

I am a teacher, and even though I am now retired from fifty-plus years of teaching high school mathematics, I will always be a teacher, seeking and seizing every opportunity to teach not only the academic lessons but also the necessary lessons of life as we interact in the marketplace of humanity. I honor and give thanks to the many teachers who—along with my parents, grandparents, community people, and even those who weren't aware of it—afforded me the incidental messages and examples that impacted my life. In so doing, they shaped my thoughts and enabled me to aspire to accomplish and to recognize the importance of being helpful to others—to be a teacher. They always kept in me the realization that there is a light at the end of the tunnel. They were always supportive as I made my life's journey traveling along its many highways and byways, its streets both paved and unpaved, its forked roads and detours—sometimes seemingly a journey in the wild.

The road map that these teachers provided led me to success and effectiveness. I now vicariously experience and celebrate their passion for teaching through the accomplishments and expressions of the students and others whose lives I have been allowed to touch and enable in some way. I believe that God works in mysterious ways, "His wonders to perform." Through His workings I have been fortunate in having many gifted and dedicated teachers during my formal education sojourn. I view myself as a composition of tribute to these teachers, written by collecting from their many attributes. Consciously and unconsciously, I am them—in this way they still live. I am one among their footprints cast in the sands of time. Because of their examples and their impact in my life and career involvement, they will contribute even to future generations.

The teachers of whom I speak played many parts in my life: role models, friends, counselors, substitute or surrogate parents, mentors, confidants, motivators, information givers, and sources of affirmation. They were kind, firm, fair, understanding, dedicated, empathetic, knowledgeable, respectful and respected, responsible and responsive, challenging, well dressed in proper attire, and professional, tactful, and sensitive as they interacted with their peers, students, parents, and other adults. They made their students feel and know that they loved them, that they were interested in their welfare, and that they believed all students could and must learn—regardless of one's station in life. These teachers of mine exercised every option and feasible positive strategy to effect in their students the development of positive self-concepts, belief in themselves, awareness of their potential, academic achievements, and "whole personness." Each teacher was unique in his or her own personality, characteristics, appearance, mannerisms— in the totality of their being a teacher.

I suppose I must have come along when great teachers were the rule rather than the exception. I can attest to this by saying truthfully that I remember, to this day, the names of every teacher I have ever had. They were most impressive, each in his or her own way, and left something positive with me that has not been erased by the clouds of time or by life's many encounters. They seemingly viewed their teaching as a ministry and, likewise, I have viewed my teaching as such. As a tribute to all of them, I say, "To God be the glory!"

I am writing about the days of total segregation and discrimination against Blacks by whites, the days of great inequity in all transactions and social experiences involving Blacks and whites. This was an era of inescapable subscription by the oppressed to the oppressor's prescription for perpetration and perpetuation of the oppression of people of color. It was before the "relief valve on the tank of oppression" had been somewhat released. It was the "back of the bus" days, the colored-only and white-only days. It was before the sit-ins, the marches and peaceful demonstrations, the riots, the boycotts, mass meetings, when schools, students, teachers, and the whole society were victimized.

Back then Black teachers were supplied with only a classroom, chalk, and erasers, but they used their creativity along with their personal monies to benefit their students by purchasing teaching aids and other ancillary materials. Many Black teachers reached out to provide students in need of school supplies and personal items like shoes, lunches, and clothes. Students had to purchase all of their textbooks and pay rental fees for the in-class use of the one set of Shakespeare's plays and other literature classics that were allotted to each teacher. No free textbooks or waivers of fees were furnished. However, even in this era of segregation and discrimination and even though there was intentional neglect at city, state, and national levels, the schools, teachers, students, parents, and communities (the whole village) worked together to provide quality education for Black students. This was before the evolution of such code words as "project," "ghetto," "urban," and "inner city" had infected the psyche of all segments of the populace—an oppressive code language craftily and expeditiously designed to communicate the negative messages that would demean and roadblock progress toward the equitable recognition, acceptance, and treatment of people of color. But still, excellence and quality abounded, especially in the education we received. The proof of this is validated by the fact that students of that era have made great contributions in every sphere of societal endeavor worldwide. All segments of society have benefited.

Teachers of that day were even denied the opportunity of having a supportive community of immediate family with whom they could share their trials and tribulations, their wins and losses, their daily frustrations, their need for positive strokes, their need for family anchorage—by law, teachers could not be married at this time. Amid all of this, our teachers made us feel proud of ourselves, our schools, our teachers, our communities, and they kept us on the "wanting to be somebody" track, as people would say then. We wanted to be like them—they served as role models.

I honor and thank those teachers who, with their caring and sharing, love, dedication, knowledge, and professionalism, played such an important part in the sculpting of *me*. I have been a successful and effective parent, educator, and contributing and participating citizen in the world community because of them.

🕸 Angela Davis

From Angela Davis: An Autobiography

During my second year at Brandeis, I had picked up *Eros and Civilization* by Herbert Marcuse and had struggled with it from beginning to end. That year he was teaching at the Sorbonne. When I arrived in Paris the following year, he was already back at Brandeis, but people were still raving about his fantastic courses. When I returned to Brandeis, the first semester of my senior year was so crowded with required French courses that I could not officially enroll in Marcuse's lecture series on European political thought since the French Revolution. Nevertheless, I attended each session, rushing in to capture a seat in the front of the hall. Arranged around the room on progressively higher levels, the desks were in the style of the UN General Assembly room. When Marcuse walked onto the platform, situated at the lowest level of the hall, his presence dominated everything. There was something imposing about him which evoked total silence and attention when he appeared, without his having to pronounce a single word. The students had a rare respect for him. Their concentration was not only total during the entire hour as he paced back and forth while he lectured, but if at the sound of the bell Marcuse had not finished, the rattling of papers would not begin until he had formally closed the lecture.

One day, shortly after the semester began, I mustered up enough courage to put in a request for an interview with Marcuse. I had decided to ask him to help me draw up a bibliography on basic works in philosophy. Having assumed I would have to wait for weeks to see him, I was surprised when I was told he would be free that very afternoon.

From afar, Marcuse seemed unapproachable. I imagine the combination of his stature, his white hair, the heavy accent, his extraordinary air of confidence, and his wealth of knowledge made him seem ageless and the epitome of a philosopher. Up close, he was a man with inquisitive sparkling eyes and a fresh, very down-to-earth smile.

Trying to explain my reasons for the appointment, I told him that I intended to study philosophy in graduate school, perhaps at the university in Frankfurt, but that my independent reading in philosophy had been unsystematic—without regard for any national or historical relations. What I wanted from him—if it was not too much of an imposition—was a list of works in the sequence in which I ought to read them. And if he gave me permission, I wanted to enroll in his graduate seminar on Kant's *Critique of Pure Reason*.

"Do you really want to study philosophy?" Professor Marcuse asked, slowly and placing emphasis on each word. He made it sound so serious and so profound—like an initiation into some secret society which, once you join, you can never leave. I was afraid that a mere "yes" would ring hollow and inane.

"At least, I want to see if I am able," was about the only thing I could think of to answer.

"Then you should begin with the Pre-Socratics, then Plato and Aristotle. Come back again next week and we will discuss the Pre-Socratics."

✧ Vita L. Jones
Dr. McAllister

Dr. Winston K. McAllister came to the first class session
wearing a beige corduroy jacket with suede elbow
patches. He lost no time presenting himself as a professor
who had little patience with arrogance and even less with disconnection from the community. Our goal as students, he
explained, would be to learn to pursue healthy lifelong learning and to translate our intelligence into consciousness, our
knowledge of a discipline into formulas for collective survival.
He railed against the superiority of "educated people," repeating again and again that from those to whom much is
given, much is expected. In each lecture he lifted this philosophy to such a high level of passion that we began to believe it
had issued from our own consciousness.

I was a prime candidate for his lessons. As a native of Seattle, Washington, I believed I was superior to people from the
South and certainly superior to students at a historically Black
college. Dr. McAllister's lectures divested me of my arrogance
and helped me see my connectedness to people with whom I
lived and studied at Howard University. From him I learned
how illogical it is to see education as a sea wall rather than an
aqueduct and culvert. For him learning was value-added and,
as a result, transforming. Dr. McAllister transformed me! He
taught me the joy of giving back as we reach forward; of finding
solutions to problems for the collective good rather than for
personal aggrandizement. The class was Principles of Reason-
ing, but it could well have been Life 101.

His influence on my life has been lasting. I am now a college teacher and when my students ask me what critical thinking will do for them, I hear myself repeating what became a mantra in Dr. McAllister's class: "It will make you participatory members of the collective of humanity. You will be of some use to yourself and to all of us."

⛘ Maya Angelou

From I Know Why the Caged Bird Sings

George Washington High School was the first real school I attended. My entire stay there might have been time lost if it hadn't been for the unique personality of a brilliant teacher. Miss Kirwin was that rare educator who was in love with information. I will always believe that her love of teaching came not so much from her liking her students but from her desire to make sure that some of the things she knew would find repositories so that they could be shared again.

She and her maiden sister worked in the San Francisco city school system for over twenty years. My Miss Kirwin, who was a tall, florid, buxom lady with battle-ship-gray hair, taught civics and current events. At the end of a term in her class our books were as clean and the pages as stiff as they had been when they were issued to us. Miss Kirwin's students were never or very rarely called upon to open textbooks.

She greeted each class with "Good day, ladies and gentlemen." I had never heard an adult speak with such respect to teenagers. (Adults usually believe that a show of honor diminishes their authority.) "In today's *Chronicle* there was an article on the mining industry in the Carolinas [or some such distant subject]. I am certain that all of you have read the article. I would like someone to elaborate on the subject for me."

After the first two weeks in her class, I, along with all the other excited students, read the San Francisco papers, *Time* magazine, *Life,* and everything else available to me. . . . There were no favorite students. No teacher's pets. If a student pleased her during a particular period, he could not count on special treatment in the next day's class, and that was as true the other way around. Each day she faced us with a clean slate and acted as if ours were clean as well. Reserved and firm in her opinions, she spent no time in indulging the frivolous. . . .

She was stimulating instead of intimidating. Where some of the other teachers went out of their way to be nice to me—to be "liberal" with me—and others ignored me completely, Miss Kirwin never seemed to notice that I was Black and therefore different. I was Miss Johnson and if I had the answer to a question she posed I was never given any more word than "Correct," which was what she said to every other student with the correct answer.

Years later when I returned to San Francisco I made visits to her classroom. She always remembered that I was Miss Johnson, who had a good mind and should be doing something about it. I was never encouraged on those visits to loiter or linger about her desk. She acted as if I must have had other visits to make. I often wondered if she knew she was the only teacher I remembered.

David L. Collins

If You Can Read This . . . A Letter of
Thanks to One of the Great Teachers

The sound of the gun signaled the end of the first half of the homecoming football game of 1970 at tiny Shelbyville High in East Texas. Even though the autumn air was a bit crisp, we recent alumni were warmed by the return visit to our campus and by the prospect of our team winning the contest in the second half.

Having developed quite an appetite from watching such a physical endeavor as football, another alumnus and I decided to head toward the concession stand for the traditional Coke and indigestible hot dog. As we left our seats we noticed, almost at the same time, that our former high school English teacher, Mrs. Hagler, was seated high aloft the bleachers near the top row. At this point, my companion turned to me and said, half-seriously, half-jokingly, "I would go up and speak with Mrs. Hagler, but I'm afraid she would have me diagram a sentence."

The statement revealed more about Mrs. Hagler's teaching than about my friend's ineptitude for diagramming sentences. I began to reflect.

Mrs. Hagler was one of those dedicated teachers who was most often described by students as strict. That she was. Her style was structured; she drew the most from students, allowing little room for student error. She expected quality from her students' work, and she got it. Students foolish enough not to complete homework assignments were few. She had a way about her that made students prefer homework over the silent judgment given them in class. She never asked that her students learn, she demanded that they do so. And out of all this came that elusive student response every teacher should elicit: *respect*. But was this lady a human being? Could she feel what everybody else felt and still be Mrs. Hagler?

I remember a bright November morning in 1964. The school's narrow hallways were beginning to crowd with students rushing to class. Someone's transistor radio was pumping the Supremes' "Baby Love" into the air, and all of the sophomore class had their English homework ready. We all wished that Mrs. Hagler would give us a break and go easy on us, but since that had never happened in the past, no one expected it to happen today. By the time class rolled around, fate changed all that.

Several high school students out for a noontime recreational drive met with disaster: a head-on collision killing three and seriously injuring two others. The entire school was in shock.

Shortly after the devastating news, it was time for English class, and, after all, English grammar must go on. But, as Mrs. Hagler entered the room, we all saw her in a different light. A tear seemed to glisten in her eye as she turned and stared out the window. English grammar *could* wait. Not a word was spoken by anyone that day. None had to be. For some reason we all understood, and we began to see the human side of our teacher.

A teacher of unquestionable integrity, she was a lady. For the background she gave me in literature and grammar, I could never repay her. A perfectionist, a lady, a human being, a master teacher—she was all of these.

This brings me to a point. In my own teaching at the college level, I stress to my teacher education students that one cause of teacher burnout is the lack of feedback from former students. Consequently, I suggest that everyone pick a former teacher whom he/she admires and tell that teacher how much his/her efforts are appreciated. This gives the teacher positive feedback and reinforcement to stay in the profession.

But, one should practice what one preaches. When I first began to work on this article, I saw it as a tribute to Mrs. Hagler. I envisioned myself going up to her door to tell her what she may never have suspected—that she was an inspiration to me—and asking her permission to write an article about her. I never got the chance. Or shall I say, I never took the chance when I had it? Mrs. Hagler died before I told her.

There's a bumper sticker that reads, "If you can read this, thank a teacher." There *should* be one that reads, "If you had good teachers, *tell* them!" I feel that Mrs. Hagler has helped me write this very article. Her incessant drills over conjugation, sentence diagramming, and figures of speech have paid off for many of us over the years. She was the best, and that's no hyperbole!

&. Lyndall Stanley
Vida Freeze

Her name was Vida Freeze. I don't exactly remember her features. She wore her brown hair piled on top of her head. She smelled good. But most important, she always wore a smile. She widened the windows of my white middle-class world from the flat state of Illinois out through other states to each coast of the United States and across the oceans to other worlds I had never imagined!

It was 1947 and I was in the fourth grade. Miss Freeze was my teacher. She used the supplied texts and maps but colored them with her enthusiasm and creativity. We didn't just learn about these places, we were *there*, seeing the colors, feeling the weather, meeting the people, and eating the food.

One of the highlights of that year was arriving at school to find an enormous unopened box in the middle of the classroom. It was addressed to the class and postmarked from the state of Wyoming. After the last child arrived, Miss Freeze opened the box and there was a huge withered ball of a plant— a tumbleweed—sitting on the floor. We all touched it and smelled it and then took it out to the playground, where we ran around rolling it to each other. I knew I felt the dry wind of the desert in my face that day!

The year ended with a play, "Around the World in Sixty Minutes," written by the students. We created the sets and the costumes. I'll never forget the entrance of a Black classmate as he portrayed an African king! He carried himself with importance and the pride on his face was unmistakable. Some of us envied his dark skin, as it revealed him as a true part of that far-away culture.

And what was my part in this extravaganza? I was the narrator introducing and connecting all the countries and cultures. I chose a curious monkey as my communicator and made a brown laughing monkey mask to wear as I hopped and ran from New York to France, through Europe to Turkey, then China to the African Congo, and back to the United States and the Golden Gate Bridge!

I am now sixty-one, retired, and still living in a middle-class, mostly white neighborhood. But now I have friends from the inner city, mountain villages, and faraway countries. My family has hosted people from many foreign countries; some for dinner or an evening event, others for a week, some for months or even a year. In doing this, I saw my city and country through new eyes and learned nearly as much as my guests from Mexico, New Zealand, Costa Rica, Hungary, and elsewhere. If you were to look around my living room, you would see brightly colored folk art. There are Italian and French CDs on the desk. There is a Portuguese dictionary and several foreign novels on the table. Oh yes, I too became a teacher—of Spanish!

Was Miss Freeze responsible for the path my life has taken? I know there have been many other influences during my life, but she was certainly the spark, the *chispa*, that started my never-ending quest to learn about things outside of my immediate boundaries. She never lectured, yet I learned from her that all life is connected and that each thing we do affects everyone in a subtle or not so subtle way. That's a very important lesson for one person to teach another. Thank you, Miss Freeze!

E. Delores B. Stephens
Planting Ivy: A Calling

If there is one person, beyond immediate family, who was my supporter at a time when my potential was still uncertain, it was Miss Ella D. Ivy (1902–1984) of John Mercer Langston High School in Danville, Virginia. She alone, at an early stage in my life, had the temerity to push when others merely assigned, to act when others only observed, and to assist when others may have only commented. While no one in my immediate family was a public school teacher, all the elders were intelligent, alert, and capable models for inquisitiveness, imagination, and focus. They laid a strong foundation and provided building materials, but Miss Ivy later became the on-site manager of the project. Her impact came before such labels as "role model" or "mentor" became clichés.

At a time before national attention focused on females' perceived fear of mathematics, and before I was aware of a gender bias that pushed females toward "softer" disciplines, Miss Ivy was the consummate teacher of mathematics. In her classroom there was no sense that the girls were mere observers of the boys, who were expected to excel, or that the girls were only concerned with crinoline slips and penny loafers while the boys learned to construct a better world. No, the girls were attentive and active participants; we were equal under the rule of the text, the chalk, and the grading pen in the hush of Miss Ivy's room.

And hush there was. A trait that still awes me was Miss Ivy's instruction in a voice that never got beyond a stage whisper. I never heard that she suffered from vocal cord abuse or that her doctor had advised her to save her voice. I believe her speaking level was a deliberate pedagogical tactic. I do not recall her ever speaking loudly to silence anyone, to make a point during a lesson, or even to reiterate one. She did not need to do so. We not only heard; we understood what she had said. She dispensed no shame for errors, no disparagement if a knotty problem overwhelmed us, and no sense that we were failures for life because of genetics, race, or gender. She taught me algebra and geometry. I recall no fear of the subjects. In fact, one sharp recollection I have of high school is the statewide math competition (of course, for "Negro" students) held at Virginia Union University for which she selected me as a participant. Apparently, confidence was an outcome of her classroom. Competence certainly was. Her instruction held me in good stead in college math courses as well as much, much later in a computer programming course in which I was older than all the other students and the teacher. I earned an A.

Presiding over her classes, Miss Ivy was respected for her command of the material; valued for her deceptively easy demeanor, which made her approachable but that belied a no-nonsense approach to instruction; loved for her genuine concern that made us feel valued; and remembered for her pedagogy that made her awesome and effective.

I have no statistics or specific anecdotes to affirm how broad her lifelong impact on her legions of students has been. Now that I am a "senior" professor, after almost four decades of college teaching, I know that she—above parents, peers, and other professors from baccalaureate to doctoral levels, from Georgia to the United Kingdom—launched me on a path that I hope is a tribute to her. If I have brought meaning and matter to young people with whom I have interacted across a desk, I have planted ivy. As for my academic discipline, I am still mystified that I did not choose math as my major area. But Miss Ivy's way was not to cajole or dictate. Left to my own designs and devices, and always a lover of words, I chose another path.

How did Miss Ivy launch me? She made me a disciplined student in all pursuits. The mystery or seeming error of my choice of undergraduate major is somewhat debunked by a professional experience more than ten years ago. I had accepted a summer position with the U.S. Army Forces Command at Fort McPherson and found myself responsible for developing statistical reports on army schools. Thus the competence and confidence bequeathed by Miss Ivy paid off again. That I attended Spelman College, to get started, is credited to Miss Ivy. She saw something that had been missed or ignored by others. As my class matriculated at Langston, I somehow failed to focus on the next educational step. In those days a very small percentage of seniors went on to college. The Pell Grant, work-study, open admissions, affirmative action, national recruitment fairs, pre-college summer programs, campus visitations, and, of course, college Web sites were not the means by which most students learned about or financed college. Above all, segregation and discrimination limited our choices. For whatever reason, when graduation time came, I had not done the research and applications needed to select a college. No member of the counseling staff at Langston had offered to assist me despite my holding, at the end of the first semester of senior year, the second-highest average in the class.

I do not recall the point at which Miss Ivy discovered my

quandary, nor do I know how Spelman came to be the school she thought to be best for me. I certainly had not considered it. She was not a member of the counseling staff and was a Fisk University graduate. Miss Ivy went into a "full court press" to get me to take the SAT, to complete applications, to apply for scholarships, and to get ready to go to Atlanta. My sights had been set, with limited focus, on colleges in the Virginia area. I had no relatives that I knew of below Virginia. I had done no research on Spelman and no other member of my class had applied for college that far "Down South." Through Miss Ivy I became acquainted with Mrs. Wilson, the one Spelman alumna in Danville at that time. She was the wife of a dentist and a newcomer to Danville. All she knew of me came from Miss Ivy, who had become my apparent sponsor. On that recommendation Mrs. Wilson became a great help in my preparation and successful enrollment at Spelman in 1956. Such was Miss Ivy's style that she would proceed with the sponsorship without explanation, without philosophical discourse on the meaning of higher education, without reminding me that she had known my family for years and had taught my siblings (who had also shown great academic promise), and without laying any burdens of her personal expectations on me.

What has happened since Miss Ivy gave me a bit of herself is my professional history. Yes, I did thank her over the years, both by writing her frequently and by visiting her when I returned to my hometown. I would like to believe that my performance in undergraduate math classes, my being selected to spend a year and summer studying abroad as an undergraduate, my overall academic record that led to my giving the Ivy Ovation as the top graduate in my college class, and my continuing my formal education through the doctorate are all shoots from the planting of Miss Ivy. Indeed, Miss Ivy came to be the kind of planter that I hope I have emulated, and do emulate, in my long and continuing association as professor and chair with students whose growth I can help nurture. I do have evidence—letters, e-mail messages, and verbal testaments from former students—that leads me to believe that I did take a cutting or clipping from the plant Miss Ivy represents and that I have planted pieces of it at various stages in my career. I certainly hope that I can come to mean to some students what she has come to mean to me. She was a teacher greatly to be admired.

ஃ *From a Conversation*
with Michael L. Lomax

When I was in the second grade, I was a faltering reader and, unfortunately, my teacher did nothing to convince me of my ability to read, to decode, to think critically. She was malicious and mean-spirited. By contrast, my tenth-grade literature teacher was encouraging, inspiring, and kind. His name was Almond Eugene Jellison. I watched with interest and delight as he stood at the lectern, throwing his head back in obvious passion for literature and for teaching. It was in Mr. Jellison's class that I became a thoughtful reader and . . . began to understand that words are powerful instruments . . . that they are central to everything.

Teaching is about empowering students, but it is also about diminishing the student's vulnerability. Good teaching requires a generous and patient spirit, a palpable love for teaching, and an intense commitment to the subject. Unlike computers, good teachers remain in our imagination the rest of our lives. Teachers like Eugene Jellison, Michael Cook, and Jeannette Hume reside inside me. I remember them. *They are presiding spirits.*

G ood teachers bring us to life. Literally. It's as if they take us by the hand when we are unsure of just what life is, and they lead us to the fullness and beauty of what it means to be alive. I think the Latin *educare* means to bring out into the light. That's the way I feel about good teachers; that they have brought me out of a great deal of confusion and suffering and ignorance. They have brought me safely to a place where I understand and have a greater range of feelings about life. I connect more fully with it. They deserve our praise and our appreciation and our remembrance.

Contributors

MAYA ANGELOU is a nationally and internationally celebrated writer of poetry and prose. Her works include *The Heart of a Woman, A Song Flung Up to Heaven, All God's Children Need Traveling Shoes,* and the classic autobiography *I Know Why the Caged Bird Sings.*

SHIRLEY CHISHOLM was the first African-American woman to sit in the House of Representatives. She is also the author of two books and continues to write, teach, and lecture.

ARTHUR J. CLEMENT, a registered architect, is president of Clement & Wynn Program Managers, Inc., based in Atlanta, Georgia.

DAVID L. COLLINS is a professor of secondary education at McMurry College in Abilene, Texas.

JILL KER CONWAY, a native of Australia, is a noted historian, feminist, and author. She is currently visiting professor in MIT's program in Science, Technology, and Society.

LYDIA CORTES, a Brooklyn-born Boricua, is the recipient of many writing fellowships. Her collection of poetry, *Lust for Lust,* will be published in 2002.

ANGELA DAVIS was a member of the Communist Party and the Black Panthers during the late 1960s. She currently writes and lectures and is professor in the history of consciousness program at the University of California, Santa Cruz.

OSSIE DAVIS and RUBY DEE, husband and wife, are nationally celebrated actors, writers, and producers.

MARIAN WRIGHT EDELMAN is the founder and president of the Children's Defense Fund and author of five books, including *The Measure of Our Success.*

ANITA FARBER-ROBERTSON, a graduate of Andover Newton Theological School, is an ordained minister with standing in both the Unitarian Universalist Association and the American Baptist churches.

LENORE H. GAY is a counselor on the faculty at Virginia Commonwealth University, where she works with graduate students in the rehabilitation counseling department.

NIKKI GIOVANNI is the author of *Racism 101* and more than fourteen volumes of poetry. She is a professor of English at Virginia Tech.

FAYE WADE HENNING, winner of several teaching excellence awards, is assistant principal at Simeon Career Academy, an inner-city school in Chicago, Illinois.

LANGSTON HUGHES (1902–1967), a celebrated and prolific writer of the Harlem Renaissance, was author of the classic poems "A Dream Deferred" and "The Negro Speaks of Rivers" and the Jesse B. Semple stories, among others.

DEBORAH J. G. JAMES, published poet and essayist, is professor of English at the University of North Carolina in Asheville, North Carolina.

JOHN L. JOHNSON has held various administrative and research positions at the University of California, Berkeley, Norfolk State University, and Spelman College, and is now a teacher himself in the Department of Educational Policy Studies at Georgia State University, in Atlanta.

JAMES EARL JONES is a celebrated star of film, television, and stage whose many awards include an Academy Award nomination for his performance in *The Great White Hope*.

VITA L. JONES, an illustrator, teaches textile design and fashion merchandising at Bennett College in Greensboro, North Carolina.

MIEKO KAMII is associate professor of psychology at Wheelock College in Boston, Massachusetts, where she serves as director of college, school, and community partnerships and director of assessment.

ROBIN D. G. KELLEY, a frequent contributor to the *New York Times,* is professor of history and African studies at New York University and author of several books. His newest book, *Freedom Dreams,* was published in 2002.

JOYCE KING, a research fellow at Southern Education Foundation, is author of *My Soul Fitted for the Sky: The Committed Life of a Black Woman Educator* and co-author of *Black Mothers to Sons: Juxtaposing African American Literature with Social Practice.*

JAMES KNUDSEN, author of two novels, is director of the creative writing workshop at the University of New Orleans.

MARY C. LEWIS, freelance writer and editor, has received a prose fellowship from the Illinois Arts Council for the completion of a memoir.

MICHAEL L. LOMAX, founder of the National Black Arts Festival, is president of Dillard University in New Orleans, Louisiana.

AUDREY FORBES MANLEY, former Acting Surgeon General of the United States, is president of Spelman College in Atlanta, Georgia.

MARY ALICE HUBBARD MCWILLIAMS, a retired high school principal and winner of numerous math teaching excellence awards, works as adjunct math teacher at Southwest Tennessee Community College in Memphis, Tennessee.

TOBY PERLMAN is a graduate of Juilliard, a music educator, and the founder of The Perlman Music Program, a camp for young musicians.

DOROTHY V. SMITH, a native of McComb, Mississippi, is the Conrad Hilton Professor of History at Dillard University in New Orleans.

LYNDALL STANLEY is a retired high school Spanish teacher who makes her home in Roswell, Georgia.

E. DELORES B. STEPHENS is professor and chair of the English department at Morehouse College in Atlanta, Georgia.

ALICE WALKER, a nationally celebrated essayist, poet, and novelist, is the author of many works, including the Pulitzer Prize–winning *The Color Purple.*

HOWARD ZINN, a teacher, historian, and social activist, is professor of political science at Boston University and author of many books, including *Three Strikes.*

Credits

Acknowledgments

When I began work on this anthology, I was teaching at Dillard University and receiving the support of many friends and colleagues, among them Keith Burras, Darlene Clark, Charles Dunn, Donna Lenoir, Nchor B. Okorn, David Organ, Doris Sykes, Bettye Parker Smith, Barbara Thompson, and Kerrie Cotton Williams. But as everyone at Dillard knows, I leaned on the talent and hard work of Tameka Cage, Zena Ezeb, Annie Payton, and Deidre Wheaton. When I began teaching at Spelman College, I was no less fortunate. Four women — Sylvia Baldwin, Wanda Polite, Velma Royster, and Alicia Smash — saw me through to the completion of the work I had begun at Dillard.

I am grateful to the many individuals who wrote moving and compelling narratives about the influence teachers had on their lives. Only the space limits of this volume prevented me from including all of them. I have no doubt that, in the future, we will hear from four very young writers who won my heart: Lona R. Cobb, Thomas J. Mueed, Ejenenorb (E.J.) Okorn, and Jessica D. Sykes.

I am grateful in a forever way to Beacon editors Tisha Hooks, Deb Chasman, and Joanne Wyckoff, each of whom made this book finally happen.